TEAM *to* TEACH

A FACILITATOR'S GUIDE TO PROFESSIONAL LEARNING TEAMS

ANNE JOLLY

NATIONAL STAFF DEVELOPMENT COUNCIL
www.nsdc.org

National Staff Development Council
504 S. Locust St.
Oxford, OH 45056
513-523-6029
800-727-7288
Fax: 513-523-0638
E-mail: NSDCoffice@nsdc.org
www.nsdc.org

Team to Teach:
A Facilitator's Guide to Professional Learning Teams
By Anne Jolly

Editor: Valerie von Frank
Copy editor & designer: Sue Chevalier

This revised book builds on an earlier version of *A Facilitator's Guide to Professional Learning Teams* by Anne Jolly, published by University of North Carolina at Greensboro, Southern Regional Vision for Education (SERVE) in 2005.

Reproduction in whole or part without written permission is prohibited. Unless indicated otherwise, buyers of this book have permission to make up to 30 copies of handouts if they are to be used for instructional purposes as long as this book and NSDC are properly cited.

Requests for permission to reprint or copy portions of this book for other purposes should be faxed to 513-523-0638 on organization letterhead. E-mail requests will be accepted at permissions@nsdc.org. All requests must specify the number of copies that will be made and how the material will be used. Please allow two weeks for a response. See www.nsdc.org/library/publications/permpolicy.cfm for more information.

Printed in the United States of America
Item #B394

ISBN 978-0-9800393-4-4

Table of contents

Tools

Preface

"A young World War II soldier decided to take a short walk in camp the night before a major battle. Gen. Dwight D. Eisenhower approached and quietly walked beside the young man. The general's identity went undetected. 'What are you thinking about, son?' asked the general. 'I guess I'm afraid,' the young man replied. 'Well, so am I,' said Eisenhower. 'Let us walk together, and perhaps we will draw strength from each other.'"

— Richard DuFour & Robert Eaker,
Professional Learning Communities at Work, 1999

When I entered the teaching profession, a set of unwritten rules seemed to govern teacher behavior and interactions.

- You are responsible for *your* students and *your* subject. (Translation: Don't tread on other teachers' territory. You take care of your business, and they will handle theirs.)
- Find efficient teaching routines and methods and stick with them. (Translation: Find a comfortable way to teach and avoid making changes.)
- Be wary of changes in curriculum and instruction — these too shall pass. (Translation: Students and society always will have the same basic needs, so just ignore the newfangled stuff.)

This peculiar way of thinking actually made sense to me at first. After all, these beliefs were rooted in long-standing education traditions and deeply embedded in school culture. Before long, however, reality hit. I realized that — however well-prepared I felt when I entered the classroom — I needed more knowledge and greater skill to be able to help my students learn better. Instead of being cautious about making changes, I found myself grabbing for new ideas. I made my way into my colleagues' classrooms as often as I could, asking questions and running ideas past them. I was never able, however much I tried, to find that mysterious "efficient teaching routine" that I could use with students time after time.

After 12 years of teaching, I took a three-year leave of absence from the classroom to work in a teaching/professional development role. When I re-entered the classroom, I was pumped up with even more enthusiasm and anticipation than I had felt with my first position. This time I felt *really* prepared to teach! I was armed with a tool kit of strategies to deal with a new generation of students. I was ready to tackle the challenges of rapidly shifting demographics and changing academic requirements. I felt sure I had the knowledge and skills to prepare young adolescents for a complex, fast-paced, high-tech workforce. I was wired for action.

By the end of the first month, I blinked awake. Looking at my students hard at work on their science assignment, I realized that instead of revolutionizing my classroom practices, I had fallen back into many old teaching patterns. Caught up in the familiar day-to-day routines and expectations that still dominate school cultures, I found it surprisingly hard to put new routines and innovative teaching ideas into operation. While I found this situation perturbing, I was curious as well.

Why wasn't I rapidly transforming my teaching practices with flexible, innovative strategies that I knew would work better? I *felt* knowledgeable and motivated. What, exactly, was my problem? Were there other teachers who wanted to change, but who — like me — found the act of change like swimming up a waterfall?

Three ideas proposed by Linda Darling-Hammond made a lot of sense to me as I considered my dilemma. Darling-Hammond works extensively in the area of professional development. She and her colleagues made the following recommendations in a 1996 report for the National Commission on Teaching for America's Future:

- Change in instruction begins with learning new ideas, followed by planning, trying out new strategies, getting feedback, and reflecting *together* with other teachers to learn from experience and refine practice.
- School organizational patterns must allow teachers to work *collaboratively* to address student needs and to develop a shared feeling of responsibility for students.
- School schedules and staffing must create regular blocks of time in teachers' schedules so they can work *together* on teaching and growing professionally.

The isolated classroom scenario simply wasn't working for me anymore. My students needed to learn more material, they needed to learn it faster, and they needed to learn it in new ways. I needed to ratchet up my teaching expertise and make permanent changes in my teaching practice. What would it be like, I wondered, to work in a culture that encouraged teachers to work together regularly on cutting-edge instruction and personal growth? What would happen if teachers worked *collectively* to increase their capability and update and change teaching practices? Could teachers break the chains of tradition by working together and forging a new way of doing business?

The questions I posed during that time have consumed me for more than a decade, steered me in quite astonishing directions, and connected me with incredible people whose work is yielding concrete ideas and answers. I watch with excitement and anticipation as the evidence continues to pile up: When teachers regularly work together to learn more about the art of teaching, they can develop the capacity to create and deliver instruction that improves students' learning and lives. Schools can, indeed, forge new and better ways of doing business.

You are probably reading this book because you want to find the means to improve teaching and learning in your own school and believe that successful team learning can help you. Teaming is a promising practice, provided you remember a couple of things as you embark on your own learning team journey: 1) Don't look for magic bullets to make professional learning teams work — there aren't any. 2) Do *not* underestimate the magnitude of this undertaking. You're going up against firmly ingrained mental models of how schools should operate. Although there are no easy answers to the challenges of improving student learning and changing the culture of classroom isolation, professional learning teams do work.

This guidebook provides tools and information that can help facilitators establish professional learning teams in schools and help teachers who commit to this process stay on track throughout the year. This book connects you with the experiences of committed principals, school leaders, and teachers across the Southeast who started professional learning teams in their schools. They learned as many of you are learning — out of need and by trial and experiment. I share these tools and ideas in the hope that *you* — as school leaders, facilitators, and practitioners — will transform your schools into places where teachers continually learn and grow.

As you start the challenging job of creating lasting change in your school, be flexible, be ready to accept detours, and remain determined to stay the course. Above all, be ready to offer encouragement and support to teachers as they engage in the hardest task you could possibly ask of them — the task of changing their teaching practices in the middle of the daily brush fires that erupt in classrooms and the status quo mentality that often permeates schools and school systems. The real winners will, of course, be your students.

May you enjoy this adventure and find it rewarding!

Acknowledgments

Much of the credit for information and tools in this book goes to teachers, teams, and leaders in schools across the Southeastern United States who worked diligently to learn, experiment, and implement this process. Together we have learned a lot from what works, and even more from what does not work. I developed other materials from ideas that I studied, adapted, and found to be successful with teams. I therefore owe credit for many tools and procedures in this guidebook to a number of wise and wonderful people whose names and publications appear throughout the book and in the references section.

Thanks to many current and former colleagues with SERVE Center for lending their support, ideas, and sound thinking to this project. A special thanks to Dr. Ludy van Broekhuizen, executive director of the SERVE Center, for his backing and support. Brenda Litchfield, professor of instructional development and design at the University of South Alabama, provided the initial inspiration to write this guidebook and spent hours editing my early attempts. Thank you, Brenda.

Special thanks also to my friend John Norton, who expertly, resolutely, and tenaciously steers me and many others with a story to tell through the ins and outs of writing for publication.

And finally, to Chester, my support, my stronghold, my fortress, and with heartfelt love and appreciation to my mother, Rebecca Baker, who at age 90 diligently read and edited each chapter in this book, as she does all of my writing.

students. To his surprise, more than 90% of students of all levels opted for the more difficult assignment, completed it, and turned it in. The quality of the students' work exceeded what they had demonstrated on their regular assignments, and students of all levels reported they enjoyed doing the work. The teacher calculated that 84% of his regular students earned high scores on the more challenging assignment, compared with 86% of high-achievers. He concluded that, in this case at least, the optional assignment approach significantly reduced the achievement gap between his low- and high-achieving students.

Following through with the optional assignment approach, the language arts teacher reported that a higher percentage of students turned in work and their work quality was generally better when they had choices in how they accomplished their assignments.

In math classes, students worked together in heterogeneous groups to design surveys, collect and analyze data, and make class presentations. The teacher found that all students were more actively engaged and tended to take more ownership for their learning. She also provided opportunities for students who mastered mathematics concepts quickly to work together during class on optional assignments. She met with these students ahead of time and explained that the alternative assignments would be more difficult and mean additional work. Nevertheless, many students opted for the alternative assignments and performed well. The teacher felt this provided a way to reward and encourage students who did good work. In the meantime, she was able to direct more class time toward helping students who did not master the math concepts as easily.

Teachers reported their professional learning team work engaged them in regular, systematic thinking about their teaching practice so they could better meet the needs of their students. As they learned how to challenge high-achievers without simply giving them more work, their instructional strategies impacted all students' learning. Team members also reported that working together gave them confidence to experiment with innovative teaching strategies they otherwise might avoid. The team structure provided the support they needed to stick with these new strategies rather than to fall back into a more comfortable teaching routine. As one teacher put it, "A lot of this I would not have tried by myself. We challenge each other."

LOOKING BACK

In looking back on the changes that occurred during this year of heightened collaboration and support, a team member remarked: "Kids are changing. They are not like they were when I started teaching. Teachers need to make adjustments and to challenge all kids. Kids will rise to expectations, and teachers are as guilty as students in believing that some cannot achieve."

Perhaps one of the most rewarding spin-offs of the learning team's efforts was the high degree of parental satisfaction with their children's learning experiences. Parents provided positive feedback throughout the year. On Teacher Appreciation Day, parents sent these team members so much food that the teachers were hard-pressed to find space for it in their team room.

Teachers acknowledged that changing their practice was hard work and required a lot of time. Yet, they continue to find the group work to be a powerful and effective professional development experience. They plan to continue systematically collaborating, reflecting, experimenting, documenting discussions and classroom applications, and ways to improve their teaching.

The teachers on this professional learning team acknowledged that their story, as told here, is accurate but said they feel their efforts are a work in progress rather than an exemplary model. They are correct. Many learning teams are doing a noteworthy job. This case study is one example of teachers who began thinking about their practice, changing, and growing professionally as a result of working together to address student needs.

HOW TO USE THIS BOOK

This case study illustrates how a professional learning team may evolve and demonstrates that there is no cookie-cutter process for developing and supporting learning teams. The team's success depends on many factors, including the facilitator's skill, enthusiasm, persistence, and understanding of the learning team process.

This guidebook helps facilitators develop and support teams by providing a set of tools to use with an entire faculty or part of a faculty. The book is organized in 10 chapters. Each chapter features a background section and facilitator's guidelines for using the tools for that chapter. A complete set of tools is included at the end of the book. The background sections give the facilitator, who may be a principal, a lead teacher, or another school staff member, a deeper understanding of the issues involved in establishing and supporting learning teams. The facilitator may use the information as self-knowledge or to help team members better understand the process.

Next, facilitation guidelines in each chapter describe the tools for that chapter and suggest ways to use them. The tools help the facilitator establish, maintain, and evaluate a specific part of the learning team process.

Adjust these ideas to best facilitate the process for the teachers you work with. Mix and match tools from different chapters to fit your requirements. Copy the tools and use them in workshops and learning team settings. Sometimes the best use of a tool may be simply to stimulate your thinking or provide you with a better plan.

Chapters 1 and 2 establish a rationale for learning teams and provide a brief overview of the process. Each subsequent chapter explains a different part of that process. Chapter 3 suggests how to organize teams and find resources and time for them to meet. Chapters 4 and 5 guide teams in establishing ground rules for their meetings, determining through data analysis where to focus their instructional efforts, and setting goals. Chapters 7 and 8 give teachers concrete ideas for how to engage in teams' real work and how to support teams as they begin and continue their work. Chapter 9 provides tools for assessing teams' impact on teacher and student growth and for gathering data for decision making. Chapter 10 provides facilitators with additional tips and ideas to successfully support the professional learning team process.

While most facilitators follow this sequence of chapters when implementing learning teams, the sequence may vary depending on what faculties already know about collaborative work.

As you read this book, you may notice an occasional overlap of information in the background sections and in different tools. That overlap is intentional. The tools are designed to be used with different parts of the process and the information may bear repeating, especially for those not following the book sequentially.

One final note: As you work with this initiative, consider keeping a journal of the ups and downs you experience and of the insights you gain. If you are interested, follow my own journey during the first year I worked with a professional learning team. Access my action research diary from MiddleWeb at www.middleweb.com/mw/resources/ajolly.pdf.

CHAPTER 1
Build the foundation

This chapter will help the facilitator:
- Provide teachers with a research-based rationale for working in teams on instruction;
- Help teachers identify the benefits of collaboration for themselves and their colleagues; and
- Build teachers' enthusiasm for participation in professional learning teams.

PREPARE TO DO THE WORK

part of a professional learning team?

Teachers may decide they want to work in learning teams for various reasons:

A sense of urgency. Many schools now face serious state sanctions if student achievement fails to improve. New requirements for teacher quality, along with national legislation requiring that increasing percentages of teachers receive professional development, add pressure. A sense of urgency may be a strong motivator in jump-starting change — including implementing a learning team process. The National Commission on Teaching and America's Future warns of another critical urgency:

"There has been no previous time in history when the success, indeed the survival of nations and people, has been so tied to their ability to learn. Today's society has little room for those who cannot read, write, and compute proficiently; find and use resources; frame and solve problems; and continually learn new technologies, skills, and occupations. Every school must be organized to support powerful teaching and … America's future depends now, as never before, on our ability to teach" (1996, p. 3).

This warning provides three sobering reminders for teachers: (1) Accomplished teaching may be the deciding factor in whether students succeed in our society; (2) Teachers must continually stay abreast of developments in their fields; and (3) Teachers must find new and more appropriate ways to help students learn. They must engage all students in academic work that supports high achievement and help all students master challenging curricula. Because they want students to succeed, many teachers may welcome an opportunity to work collaboratively with colleagues as a way to add to their teaching skills.

Collegial support. Most people who enter the teaching profession genuinely want to make a difference for students. Too often, however, teachers' working environments isolate them in their class-

rooms, robbing them of much-needed energy and passion for their chosen profession. Learning teams can provide teachers with collegial support, build skills and confidence, and boost morale. Central to the professional learning team concept is an ethic of interpersonal caring that permeates the lives of teachers, students, and school leaders.

A method of mentoring. Regularly working with experienced teachers and building habits of continual learning are good ways to help new teachers kick off a successful career. Experienced teachers likewise benefit from the up-to-date information and ideas these beginning teachers acquired through their recent college experiences. On successful learning teams, teachers play the roles of both mentor and learner.

A way of implementing schoolwide initiatives. Teachers may also see value in the professional learning team process as a disciplined, systematic method to successfully implement a new schoolwide instructional initiative, such as teaching reading in all content areas or examining student work to drive instructional change.

Relevance and value. Teachers will likely support professional learning teams if they see that the work they do in these teams benefits themselves and their students. Once involved, teachers need to find that their efforts produce effective instructional practices they can use daily in their classrooms. When teachers recognize that students are more successful when teachers gain knowledge and expertise through professional learning team work, teachers are likely to become active, faithful participants.

To highlight the relevance and value of continual learning and working together to meet student needs, consider two swiftly changing aspects of our 21st-century world. First, diversity in our schools is rapidly increasing. Today, approximately 40% of the children in public schools come from minority groups. This shift provides teachers and students with tremendous opportunities, but also poses tremendous educational challenges — challenges teachers must face together. Second, the world that students experience outside of school shifts frequently and dramatically. Educator and virtual learning guru Sheryl Nussbaum-Beach (2008) summarizes the challenges facing today's teachers this way:

"Just think about it. … This media-rich generation of students has visually pleasing information at their fingertips. With just the click of a button, sights, sounds, and people pop, spark, and compete for their attention. They carry their world with them via cell phones, handheld gaming devices, PDAs, and laptops that they take everywhere. They are truly mobile.

"At home, many have mainline electronic media in the form of computers, TV, and collaborative video games they play with users around the world whom they have never met. Everywhere they go in society, technology beckons: kiosks, ATMs, Wal-Mart, even church. The future is rushing at them full speed ahead. Until they enter the learning zone, that is … our classrooms. There, time seems to stands still. They are required to check all the communication devices at the door, typically sit in rows and columns, are encouraged to work individually on assignments. For some, school is akin to culture shock!

"Being literate in this future will certainly involve the ability to read, write, and do basic math. However, the concept of literacy in the 21st century will be far richer and more comprehensive than the education you and I received growing up. Today's students are changing. They learn naturally in social networks and through passion-based assignments that align with teacher-selected objectives (and state standards) but are delivered in an inquiry-driven design.

"Want to motivate students and teachers? Want to keep your school from becoming irrelevant in your students' lives? Start looking closer at redesigning teaching and learning for 21st-century students. We are the first generation of teachers preparing our students for jobs that haven't even been invented yet. This is tough! How do we begin with the end in mind if we do not know what the end will be? There are 21st-century skills that these kids will need that you and I never did. Are we preparing them for their future or our present?"

The 21st-century world and its myriad challenges for teaching and learning present an opportunity for teachers to turn to professional learning teams to work together to find solutions. The success of even a single learning team, when properly shared and showcased, can trigger a domino effect as more and more teachers grasp "what's in it for me." In time, "what's in it for me" may change to "what's in it for *us*, as a faculty and as a school."

Over the next decade, student success will hinge increasingly on teachers becoming continual learners and constantly retooling their knowledge, expertise, and instruction. How can you help teachers recognize and appreciate that working together in learning teams is a powerful and effective way to meet these demands? The first step is to build a foundation for collaboration by providing teachers with opportunities and information to answer four basic questions:

1. *Why do we need to continually improve and adapt our instruction?*
2. *Why should we work in professional learning teams to do this?*
3. *How can working together on instruction make a difference for us?*
4. *How can working together on instruction make a difference for our students?*

The Chapter 1 Facilitation Guide and tools can assist you with this task.

Chapter 1 facilitation guide

These tools are designed to engage teachers in exploring the purpose of collaboration, the value of learning together, and the difference learning communities may make for their students. Use these tools to help teachers gain an understanding of and enthusiasm for working together in professional learning teams. These tools include checklists, readings, discussion, and role-play. Rather than trying to use all of these tools, select the one or two that are most appropriate for the teachers you are working with.

In selecting tools, consider your audience. What do they already know and believe about collaboration, and how much time, if any, will you need to spend building a foundation for implementing learning teams? Also consider the size of your audience, the setting, and amount of time available. For example, for a large audience, teachers will ideally be seated in groups at tables. Select tools that involve groups in working together, and allow enough time for all the participants to complete the activities.

This guide explains each tool and suggests a method for using that tool with groups of teachers. Most tools contain one or more questions for reflection. As an alternative to the suggested procedures, you may give teachers a moment to complete the activity and reflect quietly, and then ask them to discuss their reflections with a partner or a small group.

TOOL 1.1 WHAT DO *I* KNOW? WHAT DO *WE* KNOW?

Use this tool to help teachers understand when working together can generate more information and accomplish more than working alone. This tool can help participants engage in a brief problem-solving activity that builds knowledge through collaboration.
- Distribute a copy of this tool to each partici-

TOOLS
1.1 What do *I* know? What do *we* know?
1.2 Think about your professional learning
1.3 Look at teacher needs
1.4 Will collaboration work?
1.5 Quick quiz
1.6 Focus questions
1.7 What does the research say?

pant. Give participants three to five minutes to individually jot down responses to the questions on the activity.
- Ask teachers to work in groups of three to four and share their answers. As they share, ask each participant to make note of additional ideas and information he or she hears from others.
- Ask participants what value they see in group sharing. Some may share that not only do group members gain new information and insight, but all members now have the same information.
- Ask teachers to suggest what value teamwork might have for them personally. What value could it have for their school's instructional program? If teachers find it difficult to see the value of collaboration for the school's overall instruction, you may offer suggestions, such as working together to build knowledge, asking questions, investigating, and seeking solutions for students' learning problems.

TOOL 1.2 THINK ABOUT YOUR PROFESSIONAL LEARNING

Use this tool to introduce teachers to some research-based standards for quality professional learning and to make them aware that professional learning teams can address each of these standards.
- Distribute a copy of this tool to each participant. Ask each participant to place an X on the line

beside each statement to indicate to what degree this description is true of the professional learning and growth they take part in. *No* means the statement does not apply to their experience at all. *Yes* means it is a completely accurate description.

- Give participants three to five minutes to indicate how they think their current professional learning measures up.

- Allow time for teachers to briefly "pair and share" and to discuss their responses. If they are participating in a small group of three to four, teachers may discuss their responses as a group.

- When teachers complete this activity, link each of these descriptors to quality professional learning. Discuss how, when properly implemented, professional learning teams can address all of these areas.

TOOL 1.3 LOOK AT TEACHER NEEDS

Use this tool to help teachers think about personal and professional needs at their school and how professional learning teams might address these needs.

- Ask teachers to place a check mark beside all sentences that apply to their situation.

- When teachers have completed the activity, ask each one to select and share aloud what she considers to be her school's top three needs.

- Keep track of participants' responses as a way to determine what the faculty sees as its greatest needs. For a quick way to determine which needs the faculty sees as most pertinent, write the numbers 1 through 12 down the left side of a sheet of chart paper. Give each teacher three colorful, adhesive-backed dots. Ask teachers to place one dot beside the number of each of their top three areas of concern.

- After identifying the top concerns for the faculty,

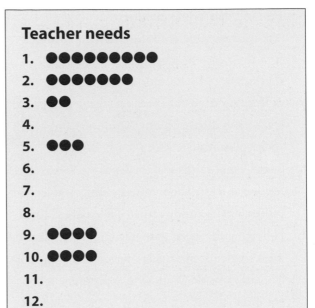

Teacher needs
1. ●●●●●●●●●
2. ●●●●●●●●
3. ●●
4.
5. ●●●
6.
7.
8.
9. ●●●●
10. ●●●●
11.
12.

lead a discussion of how professional learning teams might provide a vehicle to help them meet all of those needs. Use the tools and background in Chapter 2 to help teachers learn more about how learning teams meet these needs.

TOOL 1.4 WILL COLLABORATION WORK?

This activity involves teachers in thinking about how professional learning teams might work in their schools and about barriers that might need to be addressed. It will also provide information on what faculty members see as important for making professional learning teams work in their school.

- Duplicate and cut apart the cards.

- Ask teachers to work in self-selected teams of four or five.

- Provide each team with chart paper and markers.

- Give each team one card. (Try to distribute the two different cards so there is an even number among teams.)

- After each team finishes brainstorming, ask the teams to have one member report on the team's ideas. List the ideas from "Design Inc." on one piece of chart paper and the ideas from "Sabotage Inc." on a different sheet.

- Ask teachers to refer to the charts and discuss how their current school culture and organization might facilitate and/or hinder the success of learning teams. If you have a large group, ask teachers to discuss this in their teams and have a spokesperson share with the whole group.

- Suggest that teams make a list of the things needed at their school to successfully implement professional learning teams. Collect these lists.

- Following the work session, compile and distribute a single list of teachers' ideas for making collaboration work. Work with appropriate school personnel to address as many of these concerns and suggestions as possible.

TOOL 1.5 QUICK QUIZ

This tool can be used to generate interest in and discussion about the article, "What does the research say?," available as Tool 1.7. The quiz also can be used as a tool to summarize and discuss with participants after they read the article. Answers for the multiple choice questions can be found in the article. The answers are: 1-b; 2-c; 3-a; 4-a; 5-a; 6-c; 7-c.

TOOL 1.6 FOCUS QUESTIONS

Use this tool with Tool 1.7 to give teachers a focus for reading the article and to help them answer four basic questions about the need for and the benefits of professional collaboration. Prepare a copy of the cards for each group of four teachers. Use the questions as suggested in the instructions for Tool 1.7.

TOOL 1.7 WHAT DOES THE RESEARCH SAY?

This handout provides teachers with research-based information on the importance of continually improving teaching expertise and the need for ongoing, team-based, job-embedded professional learning

and growth. One of these ideas may work for helping teachers read and process this information.

Jigsaw approach
- Distribute a copy of this article to each teacher to provide research-based information about collaboration.

- Use a jigsaw approach to engage teachers in this material. Ask teachers to form expert groups by counting off using numbers one through three. Ask all number ones to go to one area of the room, all number twos to meet together in another area, and so on.

- Ask each group to read the section of "What does the research say?" that corresponds to their number. (For example, all number ones would read Part 1.) Explain that all groups should read Part 4 in addition to their assigned reading. Ask teachers to select key ideas from their reading and, when all group members have finished reading, to share these in their expert groups.

- Ask all teachers to form new groups. Be sure that each new group has a member from each expert group. Invite each team member to share the big ideas from his or her expert group so that all group members have an overview of the entire article.

- Distribute a set of focus questions (Tool 1.6) to each group and ask them to answer these questions, using information from the article they read. If time permits, ask group volunteers to share answers to the focus questions with the entire group.

Standing rotation approach
- Distribute a copy of this article to each teacher, along with a copy of the focus questions and a highlighter. Ask each teacher to scan the article and highlight answers to the focus questions as he or she reads.

- When teachers are through with the assignment, invite them to stand, look for some other teachers that they interact with infrequently, and get together in groups of three or four to discuss their focus question findings and ideas. After several minutes, ask teachers to rotate and form different groups to discuss the focus questions. If you are working with a large group of teachers, you may want to suggest a third rotation so that teachers meet with as many different colleagues as possible and get a variety of ideas.

- Invite teachers to be seated. Ask volunteers to share one reason they believe that working in professional learning teams will be a valuable experience.

CHAPTER 2

Preview the process

This chapter will help the facilitator:
- Clarify the difference between learning team meetings and other types of team meetings; and
- Provide teachers with an overview of the professional learning team process.

Every professional in the building must engage with colleagues in the ongoing exploration of three crucial questions that drive the work of those within a professional learning community: 1) What is it we want all students to learn? 2) How will we know when each student has learned it? 3) How will we respond when a student does not learn?

— Paraphrased from *Whatever It Takes: How Professional Learning Communities Respond When Kids Don't Learn,* by Richard DuFour, Rebecca DuFour, Robert Eaker, & Gayle Karhanek, 2004

BACKGROUND

Teachers in your school already may work in school-based teams and committees. Groups of teachers may meet to plan specific school activities, develop the school improvement plan, or help with a special school initiative. Perhaps teachers in your school also plan together as departments.

As groups prepare to meet in learning teams, questions may flash through teachers' minds or even be asked aloud.

How is our professional learning team work going to be different from any other teacher meeting? Don't we work together already?

To answer those questions, teachers might consider the purpose and outcomes of meetings in which they now participate. In typical meetings, teachers gather to plan department activities, work on discipline issues, discuss logistics for school events, address school improvement issues, or work on planning a unit. The focus of these traditional meetings might shift from week to week, and meetings frequently address several different topics.

Professional learning team meetings, on the other hand, have one primary purpose: improved teaching and learning in an area of identified student need. In professional learning teams, teachers maintain an undeviating focus on studying, learning, and becoming better teachers. These meetings are about teacher professional learning and growth. The reason for meeting is simple: Better teaching results in better student learning.

Both teachers and school leaders need to understand that learning teams are a means to an end. The aim is *not* to develop professional learning teams. The purpose is to provide a way for teachers to become increasingly accomplished instructors for the ultimate benefit of students.

Before beginning the professional learning team process, help teachers understand what the process looks like. What's the added value of learning team meetings?

Chapter 2 tools clarify the purposes of professional learning teams and give teachers information about the process. Additional information about professional learning team activities is in the Facilitation Guide at the end of this chapter.

PROFESSIONAL LEARNING TEAM BASICS

Today's emphasis on student achievement has propelled teacher collaboration onto center stage as a way to help teachers gain additional skills to help students succeed. While a variety of structures engage teachers in collaborative learning and action, the fundamentals of professional learning teams suggest:

- Teams are the vehicles for teacher professional growth and ongoing learning focused on effective classroom instruction.
- Teams develop a shared goal based on student

> **"Effective schoolwide change and enhanced student learning require a structure or a process for greater collaboration among teachers."**
> — Carlene Murphy & Dale Lick, *Whole-Faculty Study Groups: A Powerful Way to Change Schools and Enhance Learning*, 1998

needs as determined by a variety of data and information.

- Teams meet regularly throughout the school year and use an organized approach to guide their work.
- Team members rotate roles and responsibilities.
- Team activities revolve around a decision-making cycle that engages teachers in questioning, studying, reflecting, planning, experimenting, monitoring, revising, and assessing instructional effectiveness and student progress.
- Teams establish multiple channels for regular communication and sharing among school faculty, other educators, and other stakeholders.

What activities are appropriate for professional learning team meetings? The answer is a wide range of activities, from looking at data to identify needs, examining research-based strategies for addressing these needs, planning and implementing new ways of teaching, observing and supporting one another in changing teaching practices, monitoring student responses and progress, and adjusting instruction as needed.

THE MAGNITUDE OF CHANGE

In introducing teachers to information about professional learning teams, keep in mind that formidable foe — years of ingrained and accepted practice in isolation. Morton Inger (1993) notes: "By and large ... teacher collaboration is a departure from existing norms, and in most schools, teachers are colleagues in name only. They work out of sight and sound of one another, plan and prepare their lessons and materials alone, and struggle on their own to solve their instructional, curricular, and management problems." Conflicts between the current way of doing business in schools and collaborative initiatives may limit implementation, effectiveness, and ultimately, sustainability of professional learning teams.

Expect that change may be difficult and slow; after all, people like to continue doing what they know how to do. When new initiatives threaten the status quo, the change may meet with skepticism or objection. Just because collaboration is a good idea does not mean it happens automatically. The collaboration must be purposeful, planned, and structured into administrators' and teachers' regular workday (Gideon, 2002).

TYPES OF COLLABORATION

Teachers may feel that they already engage in regular collaborative activities, and they generally may — to a degree. Many experience at least four types of collaboration with regard to teaching and instructional practices:

Informal conversations. This is the most basic stage of collaboration and generally takes place in the hallway, lunchroom, or at times when teachers meet informally during the school day. While teachers may discuss instruction, researcher J.W. Little (1990, p. 6) is skeptical of the idea that "brief stories told of classrooms could advance teachers' understanding and practice of teaching." These types of conversations can, however, promote collegial relationships among the staff.

Individual assistance. Teachers generally are agreeable to advising colleagues when asked. How much this advice actually improves a colleague's teaching practice depends on the quality of the questions asked, the quality of the advice given, and the follow-up provided. Formal coaching and one-on-one or mentoring programs often produce genuine benefits and advancement for teachers. However, a coaching or mentoring program alone may not be enough to overcome the norms of isolation and individualism that pervade a school's culture.

Group sharing. When groups meet, teachers often share ideas, lesson plans, and materials with

---

AN AMAZING ADVENTURE

"The evolution of each learning team is an amazing adventure — an adventure of risk taking, collegiality, and leadership development. However, students are the real beneficiaries of learning teams. We know that powerful learning occurs when teachers are steeped in the knowledge of best practices and when they are confirmed to be effective instructional decision makers."

— *Allan Smith, superintendent, Edenton-Chowan Public Schools, Tyner, N.C.*

---

one another. Most learning team meetings begin with this stage. In fact, group sharing may even be a necessary first step in developing more meaningful collaboration. Inger (1993) notes that teachers need time to overcome years of habit and organizational separation, and sharing can be a safe and enjoyable activity for them. While such sharing is a good use of time in early meetings, without careful guidance teams may never deepen and expand their collaborative work to the next level.

Joint work. When groups of teachers work together as interdependent colleagues and rigorously examine together teaching and learning, they are engaging in mature, collaborative work. In this type of collaboration, teachers *learn* together. They jointly develop and coordinate their instructional practices. Teachers develop a collective sense of responsibility for each team member's success and feel joint responsibility for the students they teach. When this type of collaboration occurs schoolwide, the school becomes a professional learning community in the truest sense.

Although most teachers have informal conversations and often assist individual colleagues, fewer teachers regularly take part in formalized meetings that promote systematic group sharing. And most teachers, it's safe to say, do not engage in joint work that promotes interdependent professional learning and teaching. The aim of professional learning teams is to build teachers' skills in engaging in collaborative joint work. As teachers gain experience collaborating, these meetings continually evolve and change.

As you introduce teachers to the characteristics of professional learning teams, remind them that developing teamwork is an evolutionary process. As they persist and work together over time, their teams can become great resources for personal and professional growth, energy, and support.

This story from a North Carolina middle school illustrates the fluid and evolutionary nature of professional learning teams.

TEAM PROGRESS OVER TIME

When 8th-grade teacher Molli Rose first heard the news, she felt a surge of apprehension. She took a deep breath and thought, "*How am I going to do this? How are any of us going to pull this off?*" It's not that Rose and other teachers at Chowan Middle School in Tyner, N.C., didn't see the value in the new, school-wide focus on reading. It's that some of the staff felt ill-equipped to tackle the imposed challenge.

The goal of the initiative was clear: to improve all students' reading comprehension skills. Determining how to reach this school goal, however, was less clear. In spring 2001, the school decided to help teachers learn to teach reading in all subjects across the three grade levels. To help improve instructional strategies, the school used an outside consultant from SERVE Center at the University of North Carolina at Greensboro. The consultant worked throughout the year to implement professional learning teams that would focus on helping all teachers in the school

become accomplished teachers of reading.

Christy Casbon, SERVE communications specialist, tells this story. The school already used teaming and provided common planning time for teachers to work together as departments and in core groups. The principal designated one of the existing planning times each week for professional learning team work. During this designated 60-minute block, teachers studied research-based practices in reading, considered strategies that might work with their students, and developed lessons and approaches they could pilot in their classrooms.

Unsurprisingly, when professional learning teams were first mentioned, Chowan teachers weren't delighted about participating in what they suspected was yet another meeting that would eat up time. They also weren't thrilled at the idea of planning teaching strategies every week with colleagues in other disciplines. And they weren't sure about the process itself. Why was it necessary? How did it differ from other planning meetings?

Despite their doubts, the teachers gamely undertook the work. Each team comprised four teachers who shared common students. Team members began by sharing what they were doing already to assist students in reading. They looked at literature about teaching reading and decided which strategies could best help their students. Next, they chose common strategies, used these in their classrooms, met to reflect on students' responses to the strategies, and worked together to revise their instruction and monitor students' learning. The teams kept logs to document their progress, how they were collaborating, and what they were learning and doing. They shared these logs electronically with the principal, the entire faculty, and SERVE staff.

By working closely throughout the year, team members were able to focus on specific students' reading comprehension problems and tailor their instruction in all classes to meet those children's needs. The uniformity and coherence in instruction across the classrooms positively affected both students *and* teachers. Teachers reported that students seemed more excited about reading. Teachers felt they were becoming more effective teachers of reading.

Building collaborative skills across the faculty took time. "During year one, most teachers didn't see the relevance of learning teams," admits Shannon Byrum, a Chowan 8th-grade teacher. In the second year, however, teachers' thinking noticeably shifted. The faculty began to develop a sense of trust and willingness to experiment. Rose, for example, video-taped herself modeling a reading strategy in her class. The lesson wasn't highly successful, and she knew it, which is precisely why she shared the video with her team. She asked them to critique the lesson, help her determine why the approach didn't work, and offer suggestions for how to improve it. She had another motive for sharing, too. "Teachers usually see videos of accomplished teaching and don't know how the teacher reached that point," says Rose. "I wanted to show them where I started. This is as real as it gets!" She also shared the video with other learning teams who asked to see it, with the caveat that they give her productive feedback.

In the second year, teams e-mailed their logs to the entire school staff to encourage schoolwide sharing of ideas. Not only were teachers realizing the value of collaborating on instruction, but they also saw the importance of continual learning. "I know now that last year wasn't a waste after all," says Byrum. "You have to evolve to this point."

Over time, the teams at Chowan progressed from working in isolation to sharing individual strategies in their teams to working together as partners and co-learners in a schoolwide learning community. "Learning teams have become an integral part of the way we operate — a way to collaborate and learn together, a way to talk about and focus on improving student learning," observed then-Principal Brenda Winborne.

District administrators were impressed as well. "Our goal was to create an environment where self-directed learners met high expectations," says Allan Smith, superintendent of Edenton-Chowan Public Schools. "Professional learning teams have provided the framework whereby teachers direct their own focused professional growth to this end."

SEVEN YEARS OF LEARNING TEAMS

"Chowan Middle School is currently in its seventh year of professional learning teams. We have continued to focus on reading across the content areas but have widened that focus to literacy as a whole. Our reading scores have continued to rise, and last year we posted the highest reading scores in the school's history. I believe this is largely due to the professional growth that has resulted from the learning teams' focus on literacy. All of our teachers see themselves as teachers of both reading and writing, and integrate this in their classrooms on a consistent basis."

— *Tanya Turner, principal,*
Chowan Middle School, Tyner, N.C.

Chapter 2 facilitation guide

The tools in this chapter help introduce teachers to the process of developing a professional learning team. They range from a list of frequently asked questions to a skit. Use these tools to help teachers get an overview of what the learning team process involves.

This section explains the purpose of each tool and suggests ways to use the tools with groups of teachers. Adapt these suggestions as needed.

Note that some tools contain a question for reflection. Give teachers a moment after they complete the activity to reflect quietly, and then ask them to discuss their reflections with a partner or a small group.

When using these tools, consider the audience. What do they already know and believe about collaboration, and how much time, if any, is needed to preview the learning team process with them? Also consider the size of the audience, the setting, and the amount of time available.

TOOL 2.1 PROFESSIONAL TEARNING TEAM FAQS

This tool addresses logistical information.

- Give a copy of the sheet to each teacher.
- Prepare a "Holding Tank" for questions that will not be answered at this meeting. To prepare a holding tank, draw a large outline of a cylinder on a sheet of chart paper and write "Holding Tank" at the top.

HOLDING TANK

  - Ask teachers to read the information silently, to reflect, and then to list questions they have about the process.
  - Invite volunteers to describe ways this type of meeting differs from existing team meetings in their school.
- Have a short question-and-answer session. If

TOOLS

2.1 Professional learning team FAQs

2.2 Terms that describe professional learning teams

2.3 The professional learning team decision-making cycle

2.4a Table tent question 1

2.4b Appropriate use of learning teams

2.5 Meeting overview checklist

2.6a What did you see and hear?

2.6b Professional learning team meeting skit

the answer to the question has not yet been determined (for example, "When are our teams going to meet?"), then write the question in the "Holding Tank." Explain that these questions are important and will be addressed when information is available.

- Explain that the logistics for each school are somewhat different; however, the central question, "What do teams do?" generally exists from school to school.

TOOL 2.2 TERMS THAT DESCRIBE PROFESSIONAL LEARNING TEAMS

This matching activity can both help to build a common language about learning teams and serve to introduce teachers to some basic components of the process. Use the definitions provided here to help teachers discern the differences between learning team meetings and traditional school meetings.

- Duplicate the cards on colorful paper and cut them apart. Prepare one set for every two or three teachers.
- Distribute the card sets and explain that these terms and definitions are characteristics of professional learning teams.
- Ask teachers to work in pairs or small groups to

match the terms with their definitions.

- When groups have finished, ask members within each group to share answers; then lead a discussion of professional learning team characteristics.
- Ask teachers to decide which terms and definitions currently describe meetings at their school. Then invite volunteers to offer ideas for how current meetings differ from learning team meetings.
- Allow time for a question-and-answer session if needed.

TOOL 2.3 THE PROFESSIONAL LEARNING TEAM DECISION-MAKING CYCLE

This tool can be a reference throughout the year to help groups keep the professional learning team process in focus and on track during discussions and activities. Team members need autonomy in making decisions about the direction their team will take. Point out that this cycle illustrates the value of team members' professional wisdom in selecting and applying appropriate practices.

- Copy and laminate this tool for each team. Suggest that teams post the cycle in their meeting room where they can easily refer to it during their meetings.
- Discuss the cycle with teachers. Note its focus on teachers' professional wisdom and judgment and their autonomy to decide what activities will help them better meet student needs. Call attention to their freedom to experiment with new practices, the need to monitor and assess implementation, and the importance of communicating what they are learning schoolwide. Point out that the process is not necessarily linear, that teams will go back and forth among the steps of the cycle throughout the year.

TOOL 2.4A TABLE TENT QUESTION 1

Use this visual as a criterion for deciding the ap-

propriateness of activities such as those described in Tool 2.4b and as a tabletop visual to keep teams on track during meetings.

- Prepare a table tent for each group to keep. Copy the sheet on cardstock and fold it like a table tent, or purchase a box of large tent cards from an office supply store to use in photocopying.
- To use this tool with Tool 2.4b, ask teachers to read the question on the table tent. Explain that if they are unable to decide whether an activity on the list of appropriate activities for learning teams is suitable, they can use this question to help them decide. A learning team's work should be centered on activities that promote teacher learning and growth.
- Explain that this table tent also may be used as a visual prompt during team meetings to keep the team focused and on task.

TOOL 2.4B APPROPRIATE USE OF LEARNING TEAMS

This activity can get teachers thinking about suitable activities for team meetings and which activities might be better for other types of meetings. Note that these are suggestions. If your situation leads you to prefer a different response than the one listed at the end of these activities, then use your professional wisdom while keeping in mind the purpose of these meetings — to focus on teacher professional learning.

- To use this tool as an individual activity, make a copy for each teacher. Ask each to put a check mark in the thumbs-up or the thumbs-down column for each activity, depending on whether he or she thinks the activity is appropriate for a learning team. Thumbs-up indicates the activity is appropriate; thumbs-down indicates an inappropriate activity. If teachers have questions about which column to check, ask them to read the question on the table tent. This question may help them to categorize some activities.

- As a group activity, invite teachers to work together to categorize these activities. Duplicate and cut apart the activity strips. Prepare a set for every two to three teachers. Invite teachers to discuss and divide the strips into appropriate and inappropriate stacks. Suggest they use the table tent question to help decide the best category for cases in which they are undecided.

- Lead teachers in a discussion of their responses for each activity. The following suggested answers and information will help you guide the follow-up:

1. Keep the same team members all year. *Thumbs-up.* The idea is to keep teams as stable as possible. If teams meet during planning periods and their schedule changes each semester, then a new team might have to form each semester.

2. Focus on school improvement issues. *Thumbs-down.* School improvement issues generally are not focused on teacher professional learning and should be reserved for a different meeting.

3. Coordinate and improve classroom teaching strategies. *Thumbs-up.* A focus on teaching strategies is a means of improving instruction and is the heart of professional learning.

4. Keep the same focus for the entire school year. *Thumbs-up.* Teams would find it difficult to study, practice, and gain deep knowledge of ways to address a student need, such as comprehending written text, while simultaneously addressing another need — in mathematics, for example. This does not mean that teachers should not address other areas, but they might do so in department or other meetings. In learning team meetings, teachers take time to work to become accomplished in a particular area and permanently incorporate specific changes into their instruction.

5. Work on curriculum alignment and mapping. *Either thumbs-up or thumbs-down.* Curriculum mapping engages teachers in identifying curriculum gaps that may contribute to student learning difficulties. In that sense, curriculum maps could provide data for teachers to analyze to determine areas for instructional focus. However, curriculum mapping also may be a procedural task that does not involve teachers in real professional learning or growth. As a stand-alone activity without follow-up, curriculum mapping may not fully accomplish the team's purpose.

6. Examine student work and analyze student thinking. *Thumbs-up.* Working collaboratively to analyze student work is one of the most meaningful forms of professional learning.

7. Look at and apply research-based information on teaching. *Thumbs-up.* Reviewing best practices is an obvious form of professional learning.

8. Focus on classroom management and discipline. *Thumbs-down.* An isolated focus on discipline generally does not result in more accomplished and effective instruction. Learning teams often address this issue by studying research-based methods of providing effective instruction to meet the needs of a variety of learners, which often leads to a resulting drop in disciplinary issues.

9. Meet at the school and during the school day. *Thumbs-up.* Learning that occurs on the job allows groups of teachers to join together in continual professional growth.

10. Examine the impact of new teaching strategies on students. *Thumbs-up.* Collecting data and analyzing results leads teachers to a greater awareness of their practices and professional growth.

11. Include the principal as a member of the team. *Thumbs-down.* To encourage and value teachers' ability to make decisions and be self-directed, principals should make only an appearance at team meetings. Professional learning teams are a means of building capacity within the staff. The principal may support low-performing teams by briefly serving as a member to keep meetings on track.

12. Rotate responsibilities among team members. *Thumbs-up.* Rotating responsibilities builds leadership and stretches each member of the team in new ways, leading to professional growth.

13. Focus on teacher professional learning and growth. *Thumbs-up.* The essence of learning team meetings is a focus on what teachers need to learn to improve instruction that leads to better student achievement.

14. Discuss department or grade-level issues. *Thumbs-down.* Discussing department or grade-level issues is tempting, but this is not the same as focusing on teacher practice.

15. Observe colleagues using relevant teaching strategies. *Thumbs-up.* Observation with reflection is a direct form of professional learning.

16. Attend all learning team meetings. *Thumbs-up.* Teams require participation for all members to learn to collaborate effectively and to provide the benefit of their wisdom and experience to colleagues.

17. Document team activities and discussions in a meeting log. *Thumbs-up.* Records of team meetings help members both recall and report progress in their professional growth.

18. Work on procedures for improving standardized test scores. *Thumbs-down.* Standardized test scores are data to use to make decisions about areas of student need, but are not themselves the focus for a learning team meeting. Professional learning team work will affect student test scores in the long term.

19. Discuss administrative and front-burner issues. *Thumbs-down.* These discussions do not result in teacher learning and growth.

20. Share team logs and accomplishments schoolwide. *Thumbs-up.* Sharing information reinforces team members' own understanding, benefits

other teams and staff, and may result in cross-team sharing of knowledge and ideas.

21. Keep the team size small (three to five members). *Thumbs-up.* Smaller groups give team members more opportunities to connect, participate, and express ideas.

22. Study a book about instruction (book study). *It depends.* Studying a book about instruction and using it as a resource for improving teaching is great, even recommended. But teachers must apply what they learned from the book study for this activity to be legitimate learning team work.

23. Meet on an as-needed basis. *Thumbs-down.* Learning teams require regular meetings as part of the work of continually improving.

24. Keep a focus on classroom instruction. *Thumbs-up.* Improving classroom instruction is the purpose for learning teams.

25. Periodically evaluate team functioning. *Thumbs-up.* A periodic evaluation helps keep the team on track.

TOOL 2.5 MEETING OVERVIEW CHECKLIST

This brief overview shows possible components of professional learning team meetings and may help teams determine meeting activities (also see Tool 7.3).

- Distribute copies of this tool and ask teachers to examine the suggested elements of a professional learning team meeting. If teachers have seen the skit, give them an opportunity to list specific activities they identified in the skit.

- Explain that all learning teams are different and that team meetings will differ from one to the next. All meetings, however, focus on the same outcome: Teachers learn and work together to improve instruction for the purpose of improving student learning. All activities should contribute to that purpose.

DO THE WORK

CHAPTER 4

Define team expectations

This chapter will help the facilitator:

* Introduce teachers to the purposes and values of norms;
* Help teachers understand some traits of good team members; and
* Guide teachers in establishing team norms.

*"What sets smart teams apart from others is …
that they discuss and agree on norms and protocols for
important aspects of working collectively. Norms are those
consistent and enduring behaviors that group members
have explicitly or implicitly agreed to. They support a set
of shared beliefs, values, and expectations for team behaviors and determine 'how we do things around here.' "*

— Carol Beatty & Brenda Scott,
*Building Smart Teams: A Roadmap to High
Performance*, 2004

BACKGROUND

The first professional learning team meeting
should focus on establishing rules that team
members agree to follow as they work together. Teachers typically work in isolation from one
another, and meeting with colleagues on a regular
basis to share professional skills and knowledge may
be foreign to their school experience. Consequently,
teachers often find themselves in unfamiliar territory

when sitting down together to have professional conversations about their instruction and to take action
based on group decisions. Assumptions about how
to work together on a team will probably vary from
teacher to teacher, and team members need to be explicit about what they expect from each other before
beginning work on instructional issues. Tool 4.1 can
provide teachers with an opportunity to think about
valuable traits for good team members.

Occasionally, team members will bypass this
norm-setting step in beginning their teamwork.
Teams may be made up of teachers who have already
worked together in some capacity and who believe
they are capable of operating effectively without
formal procedures. Their attitudes may mirror the
feelings of this fictitious teacher in the August/Sep-
tember 1999 issue of NSDC's *Tools for Schools*:

*" … Everyone attending these meetings is an adult.
Adults know how to behave and participate in meetings. We just want to get to work when we get into one*

— initiative, creativity, conceptual thinking, judgment, special talents, and more. Data-driven schools are increasingly creative in uncovering information that can help improve student and school performance. Tool 5.1 includes examples of data teachers can use to make decisions about student learning.

Disaggregate the data. To examine students' academic performance, teams should collect at least standardized test scores, grades, and classroom assessments. Using at least three data sources for any study leads to more valid conclusions. Team members (or faculties) should then disaggregate the data by applicable categories such as gender, race, socioeconomic factors, and English language ability. Tools 5.2a and 5.2b can help teachers complete this task.

Analyze the data. Teachers may need guidance early in the process to analyze patterns among groups of students and draw valid conclusions about student needs. For example, team members might examine how student demographics relate to test scores and answer:

> **"Staff development that improves the learning of all students uses disaggregated student data to determine adult learning priorities, monitor progress, and help sustain continuous improvement."**
> — *NSDC's Standards for Staff Development,* 2001

- Do some groups of students achieve at higher levels than others?
- If so, in what areas?
- If so, to what degree?
- What are the most critical student needs across our team?
- What are the implications of these data for the team's direction?

Tool 5.3 contains some additional questions that can guide teachers in analyzing data. Keep in mind that teachers are looking for *relative* strengths and weaknesses in student performance. Even in schools where students score at or above expected levels, they still will be relatively weaker in some areas than in others. Those are areas teachers can target for improvement.

In looking at areas for improvement, team members should keep an eye out for strengths as well as weaknesses. According to Principal Charlie Coleman, ASCD's 2005 Outstanding Young Educator, gains in student achievement at his school came about as a result of changing the teaching focus from a needs-based approach to a strengths-based approach. After identifying areas of need, his faculty looked for strategies to help students use their strengths to solve some of these learning problems (Delisio, 2006). While the focus of teams is to build teaching expertise in areas of student need, identifying and using student strengths to help with this task can bring positive energy, positive attitudes, and new momentum to those efforts.

Tools 5.3 and 5.4 can engage the team in discussing data, targeting central concerns, and identifying a general focus for the team's efforts during the year. Once team members identify a focus, they will use it to craft their team goal.

SELECT A FOCUS

As team members analyze data, the data will reveal areas of relative weakness in student achievement in different categories and probably among subgroups. This information can give teams an area on which to concentrate their efforts.

The No Child Left Behind legislation suggests that schools:

- Analyze data from state assessments and other examples of student work to identify and address areas of need; and
- Identify and implement professional develop-

ment, instructional strategies, and methods of instruction to improve a school's weak areas.

Team members should make sure that the area they select is:

- Able to be improved by more effective and skilled classroom teaching;
- Important to student learning and success;
- Clearly understood and valued by all team members;
- Aligned with schoolwide goals and directions.

Some schools select a single subject area on which the entire faculty will focus. These might include:

- Reading comprehension across all content areas;
- Mathematics problem solving;
- Mathematics computation;
- Science process skills;
- Writing across the curriculum; or
- Effective approaches for teaching American history.

A school might take this approach if a significant number of students have weaknesses in the same content area and all teachers need to address those needs. While this focus may not be comfortable for faculty members who don't teach that subject, focusing all professional learning team efforts on the same content area ratchets up teaching *skills in the subject* across the school and may result in a faster increase in student achievement in that subject. (See "Team progress over time," pp. 26-27 in Chapter 2, for an example of a successful schoolwide reading focus in a middle school.)

In other schools, teams might focus on different subject areas. For example, a team of history teachers could focus on their content area, while the science teachers focus on their own content. Focusing on different content also has value. According to Joellen Killion (1998), how well teachers understand their content impacts student learning. Teachers should

continually build their subject-area knowledge and increase their understanding of how students learn their subject to deepen and refine their own teaching skills. Killion says that teachers' ability to design questions and assignments, evaluate student learning, and make instructional, curricular, and assessment decisions depends on how well they understand the content they are teaching.

In still other schools, teams may focus on teaching and learning strategies. These might include:

- Differentiated instruction;
- Formative assessments;
- Higher-order thinking strategies;
- Inquiry-based teaching;
- Looking at student work;
- Problem-based learning;
- Small-group instruction;
- Special needs students;
- Teaching children of poverty; or
- Using technology for learning.

Teams generally focus on a topic that dovetails with the school improvement plan or a districtwide initiative. Some teams choose a focus because of logistics. Teachers who meet in professional learning teams during their planning period teach different subjects and need a common focus for their learning. Many teams select a topic with strategies that can be applied across subject areas. They study and learn together, and share strategies, skills, and results. Such a learning team effort can lead to teachers solving problems across the curriculum and adopting similar teaching practices. The common approach benefits the students these teachers share, giving students a feeling of consistency and connectedness as they move from class to class.

Whether a team chooses a content or a topic focus, team members must clearly identify the specific student learning need(s) they plan to meet and be sure to monitor how their work affects student learning.

DEVELOP A TEAM GOAL

Once teams determine their general focus, each team establishes a goal that will drive members to systematically address parts of that focus. Goals do not need to be all-encompassing. For example, teachers in an Alabama school found that students were weak in mathematics problem solving. Rather than tackling all of problem solving, one team focused on learning more effective ways to develop students' number sense. After several weeks of studying, learning, and analyzing student work, the team refined the goal to learning ways to improve students' number sense by helping them increase their computational fluency. They still were on course with their original focus.

Teachers need to know that their team's goal may and should be revised throughout the professional learning team process. As team members increase their knowledge and learn more about their students' challenges, the team's work may become more targeted and the goal should reflect that shift. Keeping the goal tightly focused keeps the team firmly focused and leads to more purposeful and productive team meetings. Well-crafted goals that all team members understand and value are a key force in propelling teams forward and keeping teachers from slipping into comfort zones and old habits.

As team members write goals, they may need to be convinced that the goals should focus on teacher learning and skills rather than student learning. Some teachers may openly resist the idea. Use Tool 1.7 to remind teachers that what teachers know and can do has the greatest single effect on student learning (National Commission on Teaching and America's Future, 1996, p. 15), so goals that focus on teacher learning do address student learning. In addition, writing the same types of goals they have always written (i.e. written about student learning only) will make it harder for teachers to change how they traditionally work on student achievement issues.

The point of professional learning teams is to work differently to get better results, and goals should reflect that change in effort. When goal statements focus on teacher learning, teams have an easier time in meetings focusing on the point of the meeting — teacher learning.

WRITE THE TEAM GOAL

Tools 5.5 to 5.8 will help teams with information and procedures to write goals. Tool 5.6 has much in common with SMART goals (specific, measurable, attainable, results-based, and time-bound). If teachers are familiar with setting SMART goals, you may prefer to ask them to continue using that process. Either way, ask that teachers reach total agreement on the goal and that they include sufficient detail to provide a clear focus throughout the year. The goal should be clear to anyone outside the team.

Penelope Wald and Michael Castleberry (2000) suggest phrasing the team goal as a question, such as "What can we do differently to …?" This type of question is a powerful reminder to team members that professional learning team meetings focus on teacher learning and changes in classroom practice. Teams may prefer to state the goal as a declarative sentence. While teams vary in how they state goals, the goal should give team members a clear sense of purpose.

Consider these sample goals from elementary, middle, and high school professional learning teams:

Stated as a question:
- What can we do differently in our classrooms to improve student fluency in math computation across all grade levels?
- What research-based teaching strategies can we use to increase student reading comprehension in all content areas?
- What differentiated instructional practices can we use in our classrooms to increase the learning

of children from impoverished circumstances?

- What can we do differently in our classrooms to increase our knowledge and skill in facilitating purposeful number talks that increase students' understanding of the big ideas in mathematics?

Stated as a sentence:

- We will gain knowledge and skill in using inquiry-based methods of teaching science to engage students in higher levels of thinking and learning.
- We will use small-group instruction and other research-based methods to increase students' writing proficiency.
- We will study and learn research-based methods of sequencing and crafting number talks that foster specific computation strategies at each grade level.
- We will use research-based teaching strategies designed for gifted students to motivate and engage all students in higher-order thinking and to help them take more responsibility for their own learning.

The process of crafting a goal is especially critical since planning steps in Chapter 6 are premised on the idea that teachers have mutually agreed on the goal. If team members have difficulty agreeing on a goal, Tool 10.11 can provide tips for building consensus. Although the team may be tempted to work quickly on setting a goal, slow and thoughtful effort at this juncture will make future steps easier.

When team members have written a clear goal, suggest that teachers post the team's goal on their classroom walls to publicly acknowledge that they are working and learning together, demonstrating to students that learning is ongoing and important at any age.

Chapter 5 facilitation guide

The tools in this chapter will help teachers gather, analyze, and use data.

This guide explains each tool and suggests how to use the tool with teachers. Adapt these suggestions as needed. Some tools contain a question for reflection. As an option to the suggested procedures, you may give teachers a moment to complete the activity and reflect quietly, and then ask them to discuss their reflections with a partner or a small group. In using these tools, consider the participants. Are they experienced in analyzing data? How much time, if any, will you need to spend explaining this process?

TOOL 5.1 WHAT *ARE* DATA?

This tool can introduce participants to a variety of school and student information sources and spark new ways of thinking about identifying needs and establishing goals.

- Ask teachers to work in small groups. If they have already formed professional learning teams, ask teams to work together. Distribute a copy of this tool to each teacher.

- Suggest that teachers scan the list of data sources and identify data the school already has that may be used to identify student needs and abilities.

- Ask groups to brainstorm what other data are available. They may use the list in the tool along with other data sources they identified to help them decide which data to examine to get information about their students.

TOOL 5.2A AND 5.2B SUBGROUP ANALYSIS CHART

This tool can help team members disaggregate data, taking apart the information and looking at it in different ways. If the group is large, such as a whole faculty, invite teachers to work within their

---

TOOLS

5.1   What *are* data?

5.2a Subgroup analysis chart

5.2b Sample subgroup analysis chart

5.3   Reflecting on the data

5.4   Deciding on a team focus

5.5a Decision-making cycle for developing goals

5.5b Decision-making cycle description

5.6   Team goal-setting guidelines

5.7   Setting your team goal

5.8   Check out that goal

---

professional learning team for this activity.

- Make multiple copies of this tool and distribute one copy of the blank chart for each subgroup a team will analyze.

- Provide student demographic data and other school data from which teachers can gain information about student progress in specific content areas.

- Ask team members to fill in the name of the subgroup they will analyze, such as gender or ethnicity, under "subgroup to be analyzed" in the table header. Next, ask team members to fill in the categories within the subgroup. For example, if the subgroup is gender, data are disaggregated according to male and female. If the subgroup is race or ethnicity, the categories may be African-American, Hispanic, White, etc. The team may not need to fill in all columns since some subgroups contain just two categories. Teachers should then list the subject or other area about which they will gather data, such as reading comprehension or math computation.

- Suggest that team members refer to the sample chart (5.2b) if they need to clarify what information to record.

- Ask team members to review the available data and fill in the categories with as much information as possible about each subgroup. Remind them that they may not have sufficient data to fill in all information. The purpose of filling in the chart is for teachers to learn as much as they can about their students in order to make informed decisions about how to focus their teaching efforts.

TOOL 5.3 REFLECTING ON THE DATA

Teachers personalize the student data they examined by reflecting on ahas, questions, concerns, and the implications of their reflections on teaching and learning.

- Make multiple copies of this tool so team members can respond to the questions for each set of data they examine.
- If you are using this tool with a larger faculty group, ask teachers to discuss the questions in groups of three or four so that all will have a chance to process information and explain their ideas.
- Ask a volunteer from each group to share some of that group's ideas.
- Ask a volunteer to record teachers' responses, and make copies of this record available to all teams.

TOOL 5.4 DECIDING ON A TEAM FOCUS

Use this tool with individual learning teams or with the entire faculty, after using Tool 5.3, to help teachers reach consensus on where professional learning teams should focus their time and energy.

- Give each teacher a copy of the tool.
- Ask teachers in each group to discuss and reach consensus on the responses.
- Instruct team members to decide on a single focus for their work. Remind them that although

students have many needs, it's not practical to try to gain in-depth expertise in every area at once. For the purposes of their professional learning teams, suggest they select a single area, such as reading comprehension, for intense focus.

- If the school is implementing a particular instructional initiative, such as differentiated instruction, teams may select that topic as a focus for addressing identified content-area needs. For example, if mathematics problem solving is an area in which students need more help, teachers might study differentiated instruction approaches and select from multiple research-based options to address that particular need.

TOOL 5.5A DECISION-MAKING CYCLE FOR DEVELOPING GOALS

This tool graphically represents the stages for deciding a team goal. Since the stages address planning, acting, and assessing, the tool also may be useful with Chapter 6: Plan for Learning and Action.

- Provide at least one copy for each team, enlarged and printed on heavy paper. Or print a copy for each team member.
- Invite teachers to read through the process silently. Then use Tool 5.5b to clarify questions teachers may have and provide them with additional information.

TOOL 5.5B DECISION-MAKING CYCLE DESCRIPTION

Information on this tool can help team members clarify and understand stages of the decision-making cycle.

- Make a copy of this tool for each team member.
- Make certain that each team member can see Tool 5.5a, Decision-making cycle.
- Suggest that team members begin with Stage 1 and elaborate on actions and ideas they think

this stage includes. They can then read the information about Stage 1 and add that to their understanding of Stage 1.

- Guide teams to use this procedure to examine Stages 2-7.
- Explain that activities and assessments to help them with Stages 6 and 7 will be addressed in Chapters 7, 8, and 9 of this book.

TOOL 5.6 TEAM GOAL-SETTING GUIDELINES

This tool can provide teams with criteria for setting goals.

- Give each team member a copy of the goal-setting guidelines.
- Ask team members to use this tool as an information sheet. Suggest that they read through the information before they begin working on their goal and that they refer to the information as needed.

TOOL 5.7 SETTING YOUR TEAM GOAL

Use this tool to engage teams in writing and critiquing goals. Also make available copies of Tools 5.5a, 5.5b, 5.6, and 5.8.

- Share information from the background material in Chapter 5. Refer to sections: "Select a focus," "Develop a team goal," and "Write the team goal."
- Distribute a copy of this tool to each team member.
- If you are working with a large number of faculty members, invite teachers to work with their professional learning team members for this activity.
- Ask teachers to read the handout silently, and then invite them to discuss the sample goals with their team members. Suggest they dissect the goals for clarity and purpose.
- Ask team members to write a goal. Give them

time to look over other handouts and discuss their goal. Tell them to be sure that everyone on their team clearly understands the goal and is committed to it.

- Ask one team member from each group to move to another team and share his or her goal. Members of the other team should use Tool 5.8 to provide feedback on the goal.
- Ask teachers to return to their original teams, share the feedback, and make any needed adjustments to their goals.

TOOL 5.8 CHECK OUT THAT GOAL

This tool is designed to be used with Tool 5.7. Team members can use this tool to determine whether their goal meets the necessary criteria.

- Give a copy of this tool to each team member.
- Ask team members to use the tool to do a self-check on the goal they have written. If they cannot answer "yes" to each of the first seven questions, suggest that they revise the goal.
- Ask team members to discuss the last question thoroughly and decide on specific ways they will be able to tell that their team is making progress.
- If you are working with several teams at once, invite one member of each team to carry that team's goal to another group and share it with those members. Ask members of each team to use this tool to analyze the goal shared by the visiting team member and to ask questions to help clarify the goal as needed.

CHAPTER 6

Plan for learning and action

This chapter will help the facilitator:

• Assist teachers in examining their current beliefs and assumptions; and

• Guide teachers in developing a team plan based on the team goal.

"A good plan is like a road map: It shows the final destination and usually the best way to get there."

— H. Stanley Judd, author and producer

BACKGROUND

Once teams establish a clear goal, their next step is to create a plan to guide their journey. Throughout the planning process, keep in mind that professional learning teams address student needs by focusing on *increasing teachers' learning and expertise*. Each team will likely take a different path to reach its goal.

Consider this example of two schools that each chose a schoolwide goal of increasing student reading comprehension across all content areas.

In one school, learning team members used a facultywide approach and addressed the goal by increasing teachers' knowledge and use of research-based strategies to help struggling readers. Teams began by studying a book on effective strategies for increasing

reading comprehension and applying the strategies across classes. During the year, team members planned to work together to strengthen their use of promising strategies, to monitor results, and to compile a schoolwide tool kit of reading practices that were effective with students.

An initial plan for a team in this school might include early milestones — desired accomplishments — such as increased teacher understanding of a reading strategy and use of that strategy in the classroom. Student milestones might include increased student success in using a strategy to understand written text. Milestones for the learning team might include productive use of team time, shared responsibilities, and participation from all members. A team in this

> **"Collaboration is more than activities; it is about producing results through acting together."**
> — Robert Garmston & Bruce Wellman, *The Adaptive School,* 1999

school might decide to study a book chapter, select a strategy to try in class, videotape a team member using that strategy, and analyze the videotape during a team meeting.

Initially, the team does not make year-long plans. Members develop short-term plans with achievable milestones that help them feel successful in their first few meetings. As they continue to meet, they will see new possibilities and add activities and approaches to help students become stronger readers.

Faculty members at the second school also agreed on a schoolwide goal of addressing students' needs in reading comprehension. In this school, teachers decided to let individual teams decide their own approach for reaching the goal. Like the first school, some teams began by studying a book on research-based reading strategies and applying the strategies. Other teams planned to first determine student learning styles and then to study information on using learning styles to improve student reading. One team planned to examine student work and develop quality reading assignments targeting areas where students needed more support. Still others planned to increase their skill at creating formative assessments to diagnose and develop solutions for students' reading difficulties. Each team spelled out specific, achievable milestones for teachers, students, and the learning team and decided on specific activities to accomplish these milestones.

These two schools are typical in their approaches to a common schoolwide goal. In other schools,

> **"If our [colleagues] have beliefs that interfere with their learning new ideas about teaching and learning, and if those beliefs can actually do harm to their pupils, certainly we are obliged to change them."**
> — James Raths,
> *Early Childhood Research and Practice*, 2001

individual learning teams set their own goals. Each team within the school uses data to determine its own goal. Whichever approach a school uses, the teams' plans will reflect decisions teams make about organizing to reach their goal.

PREPARE TO DEVELOP A TEAM PLAN

The team plan is the beginning route that team members agree to follow to reach the team goal. The plan is a starting point for the learning teams' work, and also can help teachers get to know one another as professionals and build relationships. Developing a good plan requires thoughtful reflection and discussion. Team members must spend time exploring ideas, examining different strategies for reaching the goal, and deliberating on which approaches they will use. Sometimes teams shortcut this portion of the process, but avoiding planning hampers some team members' ability to contribute, limits teachers' opportunities to know one another at a deeper level, and results in team members feeling less committed to the team's work.

Reaching the goal requires that you guide teams in working together reflectively to develop a plan. Involve team members in discussions and interactions that will help them do the following:

Discuss beliefs and assumptions. The first step is to have teachers examine and discuss their underlying assumptions about students, teaching, and learning as related to the team's goal. Everyone has unexamined assumptions about teaching and learning. In fact, the practice of teaching is driven by underlying assumptions, values, and beliefs that have been passed down for decades. For example, the practice of tracking students is rooted in the belief that students learn best when they are grouped with others of similar ability. If teachers use just one teaching style, such as a lecture approach, the underlying assumption is that all students learn in the same way. Teaching can be unconsciously influenced by erroneous assumptions such as, "Some children are unable to learn because of poverty," "Children of some races are smarter," "Intelligence is fixed at birth," or "Not all children can learn at higher levels."

Verbalizing assumptions will help team members better understand one another and can lay the groundwork for more productive team dialogue. And when teachers become aware of assumptions driving their own teaching, they often are willing and even eager to learn new ways of instructing students. Use Tool 6.1 to guide teams through recognizing their underlying beliefs.

Examine current reality. Teachers next need to look at what knowledge and experience they bring to the team; they will have opportunities throughout the year to share their skills. They then examine any gaps between their current knowledge and what they need to know to successfully reach the goal. With this information, they can begin to identify areas for research and study. Tool 6.2 is a guide to help teams note and think through important issues about their teaching and learning.

Reflect on priorities and actions. Now the team can begin to consider priorities and an initial time frame for the process. What must be accomplished first? What tasks and activities are teachers likely to need to do? Team members should identify significant accomplishments or milestones to use to indicate progress in at least three areas: teacher learning, student learning, and team learning. Limit these initial milestones to no more than three in each area so teachers can reach the milestones, helping maintain their energy and enthusiasm. They may add milestones as they reach their early markers and gain deeper understanding about their work.

Teams also need to indicate in the plan what evidence members will collect to determine whether they are successfully moving toward their goal. Teams might plan to document periodic changes in:

- Teacher classroom practices;
- Student performance (classroom and standardized scores);
- Student attitudes and motivation;
- Teacher attitudes about working together;
- Team functioning.

Tool 6.3 can guide teams in thinking about and planning a direction. Teachers can use tools from throughout this book, particularly from Chapters 7 through 10, to gather information about team functioning and teacher attitudes.

DEVELOP AN INITIAL TEAM PLAN

After thoughtful reflection, teams are ready to begin writing the plan.

Writing a long-term plan at the beginning of the learning team process can be difficult because members may not understand the team's work well enough to make informed decisions about what they need to learn, what milestones to establish, and how to prioritize tasks. Initial plans need to be general rather than detailed. Early plans should focus on short-term milestones. Don't spend too much time and energy on a detailed, year-long plan since the plan will evolve and change as teamwork gets under way.

If a team has difficulty beginning to map out a plan, teachers might need to expand their knowledge base about the team's goal area. They might decide to read journal articles and books, observe other teach-

> "No specific plan can last for very long, because it will either become outmoded due to changing external pressures or because disagreement over priorities arises within the organization."
> — Karen Seashore Louis & Matthew B. Miles, cited by Michael Fullan in *Change Forces: Probing the Depths of Educational Reform*, 1993

ers, attend workshops, watch videos, or invite an expert in the goal area to work with them. As teachers learn more about their goal area, they can revisit and complete the plan. Revisiting the plan frequently is a good idea, both to keep teams focused and to refine the plan as teachers' knowledge and insight increase. If a team stalls while designing a plan, help reignite members' thinking by asking:

- What do you want students to be successful in doing by the end of the year?
- What do you want students to be able to do by the end of this quarter?
- What deeper understandings and improved instructional practices might you need to help students meet these milestones?
- What can you accomplish during your first few learning team meetings to begin to move you toward your goal?
- What activities will help you reach this goal?
- What relevant and reliable resources would help you accomplish your goal?

Tool 6.5 can help teams plan for growth in 10 important areas and keep track of how well their team is doing.

A FINAL REMINDER ON TEAM PLANNING

Finally, keep in mind that teachers' natural enthusiasm for students and their learning sometimes prompts team members to make overly ambitious plans. When this happens, teachers may later feel overwhelmed and become discouraged when they aren't successful in reaching milestones. To maintain energy and confidence, teams should plan realistically and set short-term milestones that they can accomplish.

Remember that teams should continually reevaluate their direction. Team members must be flexible, willing to reflect on their progress toward the goal, and willing to change course if needed. There are many ways to reach a destination.

Chapter 6 facilitation guide

The tools that accompany this chapter suggest ways to help teachers unpack their assumptions, recognize where they have gaps in their knowledge, and develop a team plan. Decide whether to use a particular tool based on how much teachers know. Adapt these tools and the suggested procedures as needed for the group's size and the workspace.

TOOL 6.1 REFLECT ON OUR BELIEFS AND ASSUMPTIONS

This tool can help teachers think about current teaching practices and examine what these practices say about their beliefs concerning students, teaching, and learning. Encourage team members to spend time discussing these questions to allow them to learn more about one another and begin building understanding relationships. The discussion also can help them build collective knowledge about what accomplished teaching might look like in the focus area. Use this as a team activity rather than a whole-faculty activity.

- Share information about assumptions from the background section of this chapter and discuss how teaching practices may reflect hidden assumptions.
- Give each team member a copy of the tool.
- Suggest that team members spend a few minutes reflecting on their own answers to each question and making notes in the box. Encourage teachers to look introspectively and think about the values and beliefs that guide their teaching.
- Invite teachers to share their ideas with other team members.
- Ask, "What beliefs about your students do you want your teaching to reflect?"
- Suggest that teams use ideas from their discussion to help them design a plan to bring their beliefs to life in the classroom.

TOOLS

6.1 Reflect on our beliefs and assumptions

6.2 Reflect on our current reality

6.3 Reflect on priorities and actions

6.4 Team long-term planning guide

6.5 Plan for team growth

TOOL 6.2 REFLECT ON OUR CURRENT REALITY

This planning tool provides questions that engage team members in reflecting deeply about their teaching and learning and guide them in planning a relevant and rigorous direction. Although they may not know enough to answer each question fully, this activity allows them to pool their ideas and thoughts to begin to outline a plan. Use this as a team activity rather than a whole-faculty activity.

- Distribute this tool and give teachers a choice. Team members may answer these questions individually and then discuss them, or the team may begin by brainstorming answers together.
- If team members decide to brainstorm answers together, lead them in an effective brainstorming process using Tool 4.8.

TOOL 6.3 REFLECT ON PRIORITIES AND ACTIONS

Use this tool to help team members explore ideas for actions, activities, and tasks that can help them accomplish their goal. They may not know enough about the focus area to answer each question fully, but they can begin thinking through issues they will need to address in writing their team plan. Use this as a team activity rather than a whole-faculty activity.

- Give each team member a copy of this tool. Invite teachers to read over the questions.
- Suggest that teachers use a brainstorming pro-

cess. Give team members a copy of Tool 4.8 and ask them to review the process.

- Suggest that the team select one person to facilitate the activity and lead the group through the process.

- When team members complete this activity, they should be ready to formalize some concrete plans for their teams.

TOOL 6.4 TEAM LONG-TERM PLANNING GUIDE

Teams may use this tool to help them record their plan.

- Make a copy of this tool for each team member.

- Invite team members to organize their decisions and write their team plan information using this form or in any other way they prefer.

- Remind teams that their plan should be flexible and subject to changes as the need arises, and that the activities they select should focus on teacher learning and growth.

- Instruct teams to keep a copy of this plan in their team notebook and to refer to it regularly to monitor their progress or make needed adjustments.

- Invite teams to share a copy of their plan with other teams if they feel comfortable.

TOOL 6.5 PLAN FOR TEAM GROWTH

This tool lists 10 important characteristics of successful professional learning teams. Use it to help teams plan to track their progress in exhibiting these characteristics. This tool may be used at any time during the professional learning team process and is introduced here to prompt teams to begin now to plan for success.

- Copy and distribute several copies of this tool to each team. The team will use a new form for each team growth check.

- Ask team members to review the list of professional learning team characteristics. Suggest that they talk about what the characteristic might look and sound like in practice.

- Ask teams to complete and date one growth check form during an initial meeting. Suggest that team members fill out this form monthly or quarterly and compare it with previous growth checks to track their progress in acquiring these team traits. Each time team members complete a form, they should be able to add new information to support growth in most characteristics. When they initially fill out this form, they might leave the last two characteristics blank since they will not have begun applying new knowledge and skills in the classroom or monitoring student learning and success.

CHAPTER 7

Conduct successful meetings

This chapter will help the facilitator:

*   Introduce ideas to help teachers plan and prepare for successful team meetings;
*   Give concrete suggestions for successful team interactions; and
*   Troubleshoot and ease teams over hurdles they may encounter.

"Teamwork is the ability to work together toward a common vision. It is the fuel that allows common people to attain uncommon results."

— Andrew Carnegie

"The way a team plays as a whole determines its success. You may have the greatest bunch of individual stars in the world, but if they don't play together, the club won't be worth a dime."

— Babe Ruth

BACKGROUND

When professional learning teams have reached consensus on ground rules, agreed on a goal, and roughed out a plan for the year, team members should be ready to think more deeply about how they can take maximum advantage of one of their most precious commodities: their meeting time.

No one wants to spend time in unproductive and unsuccessful endeavors. Productive meetings occur not through happenstance, but with careful attention and planning. Teams will face predictable challenges, and knowing what hurdles they might encounter can help members troubleshoot. Team members may find these ideas and suggestions helpful in steering meetings toward success and productivity.

Find the best possible meeting space. Teachers have busy schedules and frequently grab the first available spot for a meeting. Physical surroundings influence team behaviors and progress. In fact, the meeting area sets the stage for how team members work together. Ideally, team meeting accommodations include:

*   A well-lighted area.
*   Comfortable, adult-size chairs at a table or in a circle facing each other.
*   An area out of the line of traffic and free from interruptions from students, parents, other teachers, custodians, and office staff.

- Access to materials such as flip charts and markers, computers with Internet access, and other needed equipment.
- Team visuals and charts. Tool 7.15 is an example of one type of chart you may display. You might also display the team goal, team norms, pictures of team members' students, and other visuals that add interest and information.

While the team meeting area may not meet all of those measures, make it is as inviting, comfortable, and free from interruptions as possible.

> **"Conflict is a manifestation of interdependence. Without a need for one another, there would be no conflict. Conflict is necessary in order to have community."**
> — Robert Garmston & Bruce Wellman, *The Adaptive School,* 1999

Clarify identities and responsibilities. The process of building a team identity challenges members' existing mental models that might otherwise lead them into nonproductive roles. Successful team members understand their roles within the team and the responsibilities those roles entail.

Robert Garmston and Bruce Wellman (1999) advise team members to reflect on two questions that can help them develop a sense of identity on the team:

1. Who am I within this team?

2. Who do I need to be?

The identities team members develop will influence their beliefs, values, and behaviors. Understanding who they are on the team also can help members clarify productive roles they can play and may foster commitment to the team.

After members reflect and discuss their individual identities on the team, they should address who they are collectively. The whole team should reflect on these questions:

1. Who are we as a team?

2. What is our purpose?

3. Who do we need to be to accomplish that purpose?

Answering these questions pushes team members toward a sense of unity and collective identity. For that reason, lead teams to begin clarifying identities and responsibilities after they set their team goal. Throughout the learning team process, invite team members to reflect on these questions whenever they need a boost to keep their energy and productivity high.

Team members also need a sense of where they fit into traditional team responsibilities. Each meeting should have a team leader and a recorder, responsibilities that should be rotated throughout the year to allow all members the chance to build leadership capacity, share the work, and ensure that the team's continuance does not rest in the hands of one or two key people.

To help assign responsibilities, teams might set up a schedule. The group will need to decide who will be leader for how long, what the leader's responsibilities will involve, who will record meeting information, and who will gather materials or information needed for the next team meeting.

As the learning team continues to meet, members may find it helpful to take a minute or two at the end of each meeting for individuals to summarize their upcoming responsibilities: "I'll be the leader next week. That means I will …"

Understand productive teaming. Successful meetings depend on team members working together effectively. Synergy is the phenomenon in which the combined work of a team of people is greater than the sum of their efforts or capabilities individually.

When teachers developed their team plan (Chapter 6), they examined their assumptions and beliefs about teaching and learning. Now it is time for them to examine their assumptions and beliefs about how successful teams work together. What do group members believe effective teamwork looks and sounds like? And just as important — how will they get there?

Teams first may need to reconsider the assumption that extreme politeness and lack of conflict are important to having a good team meeting. Erik Van Slyke (1997), a human resource management expert, writes that the inevitable conflicts that arise as people work together can be used to create an atmosphere of understanding and trust.

Shari Caudron (2000) says team conflict is an important creative force. In successful and productive learning teams, healthy conflict is vital. Healthy conflict produces the creative spark necessary to stimulate new thinking and engages teachers in disagreements and differences over *ideas* and *issues*. As team members explain their ideas, they offer diverse thoughts and insights. Differing viewpoints stimulate deeper thinking and innovation on the part of the team. Healthy conflict is an antidote for groupthink and passivity. It improves the quality of decision making, leads to richer understandings, and builds trust and team synergy.

How teachers interact as they discuss issues determines how successfully they maintain healthy rather than harmful conflict. Conflict that becomes personal — aimed at individuals or groups of individuals — harms teams. Personal conflict depletes energy, interferes with team work, and frustrates team progress. This type of conflict needs to be stopped quickly and replaced with productive interactions. When team members follow norms, respect and listen to each other, and honor all ideas, then conflict generally remains focused on ideas rather than people. Several tools in this chapter, including Tools 7.5, 7.6, and 7.7, offer suggestions for healthy team behaviors and dealing with harmful conflict.

Practice trusting behaviors. Trust is the glue that holds successful teams together. Anthony Bryk

and Barbara Schneider (2002) found that schools with a high degree of *relational trust* (social relationships based on respect, competence, personal regard, and integrity) are more likely to make changes that raise student achievement than schools where relationships are poor. Bryk and Schneider conclude that without trust, improvements in classroom instruction, curriculum, teacher preparation, and professional development have less chance of succeeding.

The issue of relational trust needs special attention at all stages of team development. A working definition of trust might read something like this: *Trust is a mutually shared belief that you can depend on each other to achieve a common purpose.* Team members sense how others in the team feel about them. Building trusting relationships requires changing negative attitudes and become nurturing and accepting of other team members. Learning team members will learn the strengths and shortcomings of team members and must learn to accept them as they are and value them as individuals. Tools to explore the issue of trust further are in the Chapter 7 tools section.

Know how to do the work of the team. In successful team meetings, teachers join forces, target specific student learning needs, and create and apply solutions. The professional learning team decision-making cycle shown in Tool 2.3 illustrates what teams do and accomplish during team meetings. You may want to look at that tool as you read the next few paragraphs describing stages of that cycle.

As most teams begin to work, they explore studies and research their area of focus. Teachers might

> "Teams cannot improve trust. They can only increase trusting behaviors."
> — Robert Garmston & Bruce Wellman, *The Adaptive School,* 1999

look at journal articles, books, and research, observe other teachers who are accomplished at using a particular strategy, get expert advice, watch videos, and seek other ways of gaining knowledge. They compare their instructional practices with what research says they need to be doing to help their students and add activities to their team plan to fill in the gaps.

Throughout the process, team members reflect and use research and their own professional wisdom to make decisions. Members frequently question the value of specific instructional strategies, practices, ideas, and theories. They zero in on approaches they believe may increase their teaching effectiveness and look for opportunities to apply these in the classroom. Team meetings are a time to design lessons, tools, materials, and assessments around new teaching methods.

As teachers experiment collectively with new teaching practices, their plans and ideas come to life in the classroom. At this point, teachers carefully monitor and assess implementation. Team members may visit each other's classes to watch colleagues experiment with these new strategies. If scheduling makes observation difficult, teachers might videotape lessons and share the videotapes during team meetings. Throughout the process, they keep track of how students respond to different ways of teaching. The team studies samples of student work — including the work of struggling students — for new insight into problems. Teams often compare teacher assignments and student work products to determine if the assignment accomplishes intended learning goals. Teachers constantly refine tools, approaches, and strategies

> **"Success seems to be connected with action. Successful people keep moving. They make mistakes, but they don't quit."**
> — Conrad Hilton, founder of Hilton Hotels

based on their discussions and observations.

The work of professional learning teams is, in sum, a problem-solving process. Problems that can seem insurmountable shrink to life-size as teachers work on them together.

Communicate! Regular communication is *crucial* to team success. Successful teams regularly communicate their work to other teachers, students, administrators, consultants, or interested and involved people. They offer others a picture of team meetings, generate opportunities for others to reflect and provide feedback, and create visibility for teachers' work. Ongoing communication can wipe out isolation and set the school on course for becoming a professional learning community.

Use logs for communication. The premiere tool for team communications is the meeting log. A log is *not* minutes of the meeting. In a log, a team member records both the big ideas from the team's discussions during the meeting and decisions the team makes. Remind the team recorder that the log is not being evaluated and need not be lengthy. Big ideas may simply be listed, even bulleted. The idea is to communicate information that helps readers get inside the meeting, glimpse the team's thinking, and learn where the team is going.

According to researcher Robert Gable (1999), evidence shows that teams benefit from maintaining a cumulative written memory of their discussions and work (p. 183). Carlene Murphy and Dale Lick (1998) strongly recommend completing a log — a brief, written summary of each meeting — during or immediately after each meeting as a way of keeping a history of the group's work (p. 53).

Refrain from developing a template for the log. Templates generally turn into fill-in-the-blank activities. Logs give readers more and better information when they have free-flowing information and ideas about team activities and discussions.

Logs create opportunities for both teams and teachers:

- They open the team meeting room door to the whole school community and reveal learning, discoveries, successes, and concerns. As others offer ideas and input in response, a larger schoolwide conversation begins about teaching and learning.

- Logs supply a written plan (agenda) for the next team meeting. Meeting plans flow from specific tasks the team needs to accomplish. Before team members leave a meeting, their last order of business is to plan the next meeting and decide how to prepare for that meeting. All team members should have input so that the agenda belongs to all. Planning the agenda this way helps to build collective ownership of team meetings. Having one team member develop an agenda leads to that person owning the meeting. No one outside the team should develop the team agenda.

- Team members use logs to review past strategies and directions and to track their effectiveness. Logs record the team's history and can help new team members catch up on the team's work.

- Evidence in logs that teachers are regularly engaging in professional learning can be used to provide professional development credit or to meet criteria for teachers' personal growth plans.

- Teams can use logs to channel ideas and practices to others and as idea maps for the future.

- Logs can furnish data for evaluating the professional learning team process. They also are a valuable source of data and documentation for school accreditation and school improvement plans.

- Logs set up a process for communicating with and getting feedback from principals. (More information about providing effective feedback is in Chapter 8.)

- Logs serve additional functions, but their greatest value is to create opportunities for schoolwide feedback and interaction and to help build a community of professional learners.

Use technology for communication. Online networking tools allow people to regularly interact at their convenience, creating myriad ways for teams to communicate. For example, a middle school team facilitator said:

"Having several professional learning community meetings going on in our building simultaneously, I find it impossible as a facilitator to attend them all and offer meaningful input and support. Technology resources, such as wikis, have allowed me to be 'virtually' present in many meetings with our teachers all at once. In addition to being a great time management tool, technology makes it convenient for us to dialogue, make announcements, and share resources among the various professional teams on our campus. Although we share a common goal regarding student achievement and success, we are often unaware of what other individuals and teams are accomplishing in the classrooms right next door. Technology has managed to bridge the communication gap that causes the feel of isolation in the teaching profession and create among us a community of collaborators."

> — *LaTonya McNeill,*
> *professional learning communities facilitator,*
> *Douglas Byrd Middle School, Fayetteville, N.C.*

Expanding team members' use of collaborative web tools offers new and intriguing opportunities for

> **"We encourage members of the group to gather ongoing data that answer a simple question: 'What is happening?'"**
> — Penelope Wald & Michael Castleberry, *Educators as Learner,* 2000

working together with team members and other colleagues. Carlene Murphy and Dale Lick (1998) suggest additional ways to communicate the team's work to others — through newsletters, videos, bulletin boards, snapshots, slide shows, workshops, discussion groups, poster displays, and samples of activities and work designed and refined by learning teams. Teams might also invite people to their meetings and post a weekly "best idea" in the school newsletter or parent bulletin. Throughout the team process, successful teamwork will depend on successful communication.

Decide on tangible outcomes and products.
Determining a tangible outcome can give teams life, energy, and purpose. If team members choose to develop a specific product, however, be certain that the team's work remains focused on teacher learning, not only on developing products or culminating activities. Products may take many different forms. These examples of tangible outcomes have built visibility for professional learning team work:

- Workshop and conference presentations that give team members a venue for sharing what they are doing and learning through their professional learning team work.

- A school newsletter that spotlights learning team successes and presents information and ideas gathered during the course of teams' work.

- A video demonstrating some new instructional practices the team is field testing. This could become part of a staff development library or be used as a mentoring activity for new teachers.

- A portfolio of team-developed lessons, notes on the lessons' success, and copies of revised plans. Portfolios also might contain copies of research and information teachers gather.

- A teaching tool kit of information and practices to serve as a resource for other teachers, especially new teachers.

- A blog (weblog) that highlights the team's work. For example, teacher Karl Fisch created an award-winning blog for his school with a far-reaching impact located at http://thefischbowl. blogspot.com. Teacher blogging is becoming increasingly common.

Membership in free online teacher communities such as the influential *Tapped In* site (http://tappedin.org/) where team members can meet other educators and even set up their own virtual office for virtual mingling and sharing.

Since ways of working together across time and space boundaries are developing so rapidly, team members who are interested in going virtual with their learning need a way keep up with what's available. To stay abreast of online community networking, visit the 21st Century Collaborative — the brainchild of virtual learning community guru Sheryl Nussbaum-Beach — at http://21stcenturylearning. typepad.com/.

TROUBLESHOOTING

Even the most successful teams experience bumps in the road. Productive meetings may depend on being able to smooth those bumps. Some common approaches have proved useful to other teams that experienced problems. Be patient and persistent as you use these ideas, and experiment with other solutions. Remember that opportunities to solve problems provide opportunities to learn.

"We keep getting off track with our discussions."
Conversation guides are tools to help team members stay focused and on track during the meetings. Tool 7.10 uses the process described on p. 18 of *The Art of Focused Conversation: 100 Ways to Access Group Wisdom in the Workplace* (New Society Publishers, 2000) and involves asking questions at four levels:
1. Objective questions: questions about facts;

2. Reflective questions: questions that elicit personal reactions and feelings;

3. Interpretive questions: questions that draw out meanings, values, and implications;

4. Decisional questions: questions that lead to a decision about the topic.

These guides, along with the guided practice provided by Tools 7.9 and 7.11, typically can keep teams focused. Be sure all team members are familiar with the guides and know how to design their own conversation prompts. Since team leadership rotates, all team members need to accept responsibility for keeping conversations on track.

"Sometimes our meetings turn into gripe sessions!"

In a 2004 article for *JSD,* Richard DuFour points out the importance of helping team members focus on issues within their control. When an issue arises that causes griping and sidetracks progress, ask, "Is this something we can control?" Examine concerns. Better facilities, more access to technology, increased planning time, smaller class sizes, scheduling constraints, etc. are certainly barriers, but teachers have little control over these factors. On the other hand, teachers can learn to understand and control:

• Setting clear, focused learning goals for students;

• Gaining better understanding of where students are in their learning;

• Establishing a systematic plan for addressing student learning problems;

• Improving instructional practices in areas where students need help;

• Building a collaborative culture in which teachers work together to help one another strengthen teaching expertise;

• Having high expectations for students and teachers;

• Adjusting attitudes and beliefs about colleagues, students, parents.

The factors teachers *can* control actually have a more powerful impact on student achievement than the elements they do not control. When teachers gripe, refocus their attention on conditions that lie within their sphere of influence and which they can successfully address.

"Some team members don't like each other!"

The first step in liking one another is getting to know one another. This may sound elementary, but many teams mess this up. First, make sure everybody knows everyone's name. Some people aren't good at remembering names, so provide the group with a list of team members, especially if you have new teachers aboard.

The beliefs teachers hold about one another can present another barrier to smooth working relationships. We draw conclusions about others' values and make judgments about them based on what we think we know about them. Teachers may avoid working with certain colleagues because they assume that they have different beliefs about teaching, learning, and the purposes of schooling. These assumptions can stand in the way of the important work to be done: educating all students. To help with this issue, teachers need to spend some time getting to know something about one another on both the personal and professional levels. Tool 7.1 provides one approach for doing this. If some team members don't want to fill this out, you might sit in on a meeting and engage team members in discussing these questions. After all, you need to get to know them, too!

> **"A school must become a place where teachers are involved in a community of learning, caring, and inquiring."**
> — Shirley Hord, *Professional Learning Communities,* 1997

"The people in our team have nothing in common."

Diversity actually makes it possible for teams to operate with energy and creativity. Teachers often are referring only to their teaching assignments when they say they have nothing in common. Actually, they have many more commonalties than differences. Help teachers focus on commonalties. Don't tell them what they have in common. Let them decide and tell one another. Some common factors may be that they probably teach students of a similar age; they care about students and student learning and growth; they may share some of the same students; they want to be effective teachers.

> **"Fix what is broken, not what is showing."**
> — Robert Garmston & Bruce Wellman, *The Adaptive School,* 1999

Next, focus on team members' complementary strengths. For example, one member may be good at seeing the big picture. Another may be more detail-oriented. Both of these skills are needed. Ask team members to describe their learning styles and possible contributions to the team. Chart all responses so teachers have a picture of their strengths.

"We didn't get anywhere in our meeting."

This concern may be addressed by helping teams focus on what their meeting *did* accomplish. At the conclusion of each team meeting, suggest that team members reflect on their time together. Their reflection should be a fast-paced conversation that gives team members information to guide changes at their next meeting. The "Reflect on the meeting" flip strip from Tool 7.11 contains some good summary questions to use. Tool 7.13 can help team members agree at the beginning of a meeting on what they want to accomplish.

"Aren't we supposed to be getting students ready for The Test?"

Before you shudder, keep in mind that many teachers have entered teaching only within the last decade. They've taught only in situations where they were expected to focus on and fix standardized test scores. You can make several points when this issue looms. First, the learning team's job is not to fix standardized test scores (although improved student achievement will be an outcome of increasingly accomplished teaching). A focus on test scores is work on appearance — on fixing what shows — rather than work on the underlying problem. Fixing what's broken requires understanding that comes with focused study in a targeted area and is work that prepares students for lifetime success.

Next, invite teachers to work together on developing and using formative assessments — classroom assessments that will provide them with a more detailed profile of student strengths and weaknesses than simple test scores. These types of assessments are powerful tools when teachers use them to make informed decisions about ways to deliver more effective and targeted instruction.

SUCCESSFUL TEAMWORK HAS BENEFITS

Expertise about teaching and learning will grow and strengthen as teachers participate in successful teamwork. Over time, this expertise should become so embedded in the school's culture that it becomes a natural way of doing business. Robert Garmston and Bruce Wellman (1999) describe four states of mind that capable and proficient team members display. These attributes will become increasingly evident as teams become more proficient and successful:

- **Efficacy:** Capable team members believe that they can successfully improve their practice and are willing to do so. Teachers' collective efficacy, or belief in their ability to make a difference, may be the most consistent variable connected to a school's success.

- **Flexibility:** Capable team members view situations from multiple perspectives. They honor and explore diversity and expand the limits of their own thinking. They help the team as a whole build new competencies.

- **Consciousness:** Capable team members are aware of their own thoughts, feelings, behaviors, and intentions, and are aware of how they affect others. Their self-examination and self-awareness govern their interaction with other team members and their decision making.

- **Interdependence:** Capable team members recognize the connectedness of staff, students, parents, and others. They rely on one another for assistance, support, survival. Team members propel one another forward in their work.

Because of their mind-sets, capable and successful team members become increasingly skilled in teamwork, teaching, and the art of ongoing learning. You, the school staff, and your team members have a lot to look forward to. Successful learning teams build capable teachers and a lively culture of teaching and learning that becomes a part of the way the school operates.

Chapter 7 facilitation guide

The tools for this chapter offer teamwork information, conversation guides, communication procedures, progress self-assessments, and other aids to help teachers conduct successful team meetings. This guide explains each tool and suggests a method for using it.

Prepare a set of tools for each team or individual to be available when they need them.

TOOL 7.1 LET'S GET ACQUAINTED!

Use this tool to help build understanding and rapport among team members. Even when teachers see each other every day, their personal knowledge of one another may be superficial or incorrect.

*   Be sure each team member has a copy of this tool before the first professional learning team meeting.
*   Ask teachers to make brief notes about themselves on the handout and to bring the handout with them to the first professional learning team meeting.
*   In the meeting, ask teachers to share information about themselves. Suggest they begin by sharing information for the first question and having all team members comment before moving on to the next questions.
*   Encourage team members to ask each other follow-up questions.

TOOL 7.2 PROFESSIONAL LEARNING TEAM ROLES

This tool can help teachers become familiar with the roles and responsibilities of the team leader and the team recorder. Since these positions rotate, all members should understand the responsibilities and support one another in the roles.

*   Ask teachers to bring a copy of these team roles to the meeting.
*   Ask them to look over the role of the team leader

TOOLS

7.1   Let's get acquainted!
7.2   Professional learning team roles
7.3   Professional learning team activity generator
7.4   Quality indicators
7.5   The dysfunctional discussion division
7.6a Trust factors
7.6b Trust factors
7.7   A portrait of trust
7.8   Team communications
7.9   Anywhere School memo
7.10 Hold productive conversations
7.11 Conversation quick guides
7.12 Understanding Student Thinking video observation guide
7.13 Regroup before the meeting
7.14 Team progress self-assessment
7.15 Are we on target?

and to ask how they might accomplish a particular task or if that task is necessary in their situation. They also might add tasks, but caution them not to make this responsibility too labor-intensive. In professional learning team meetings, all team members share responsibility for the meeting.

*   Follow the same procedure when discussing the team recorder's role.
*   Work with teachers on details about sharing the logs. Will the recorder e-mail the logs or post them online? How soon after the meeting? Who will receive them or have access to the web site with the posted information?

TOOL 7.3 PROFESSIONAL LEARNING TEAM ACTIVITY GENERATOR

This tool can give teachers ideas for what to

do in team meetings if the team gets bogged down or confused. It also lists team activities for meeting times. Team members should review this tool periodically to focus or refocus their efforts.

- Be sure all teachers have a copy of the tool.
- Explain that since the professional learning team process may be new to teachers, teams may be uncertain about what to do during team meetings. The activities listed, although not exhaustive, can help teams focus on what they should do regularly. Teams do not need to engage in all of the listed activities.
- Suggest that team members read through the list and ask clarifying questions. They also may want to suggest additional activities, a good opportunity for you to remind team members that any activity that does not focus on systematic teacher growth and development probably is not right for a professional learning team meeting.
- Suggest that teams keep a copy of this tool in the team notebook for quick reference.

TOOL 7.4 QUALITY INDICATORS

Use this tool to give teams a deeper look at indicators, or criteria, for quality teaching activities.

- Copy these bookmarks on heavy paper, preferably colorful cardstock. Cut them apart and distribute one to each teacher.
- Explain that teachers can use these indicators when developing team activities, procedures, lessons, and so on.
- Ask each teacher to silently read the indicators. Explain that you have prepared the indicators on a bookmark for teachers to have a quick reference tool to gauge the quality of assignments they give students.
- Professional learning teams may want to create a poster of the indicators to display in the team meeting room to use to reflect on the quality

of the teaching activities and approaches they develop in meetings.

TOOL 7.5 THE DYSFUNCTIONAL DISCUSSION DIVISION

This activity engages team members in thinking about the kind of talk they want in their teams. How do team members speak with one another in supportive and productive ways that build rapport?

- Make sure each teacher has a copy of this tool.
- Provide chart paper and markers for each team or table group.
- Invite teachers to read through the list of members of the dysfunctional discussion division. They may recognize many of these individuals from previous meetings.
- Suggest that they add to the list of dysfunctional discussers. They can come up with other inappropriate ways of talking and name the imaginary individual who portrays those traits. Ask them to list any new destructors on the chart paper.
- Invite participants to assemble an imaginary team to counteract the dysfunctional division. Call it the "creative communicators corps" or have teachers come up with another name for this group. Ask them to consider productive ways of talking and to suggest a name for an individual who represents each trait. List these creative communicators on chart paper.

TOOL 7.6A AND 7.6B TRUST FACTORS

While there are no magic bullets for building trust in teams, these two tools can help teachers reflect on behaviors that build trust and gauge the trust level among team members.

- Be sure participants have copies of both tools.
- Explain that Tool 7.6a describes attitudes and behaviors that build trust. Point out that the

only way to improve trust on a team is to improve trusting behaviors. This tool gives team members a glimpse of what these behaviors might look like. Tool 7.6b will help them understand the current trust level on their team.

- Tell team members to discuss each factor described on Tool 7.6 and reach consensus on how their team measures up. They should discuss one factor thoroughly and indicate the current trust level before moving on to the next factor.
- When teams have completed the chart, suggest that they save a record in the team notebook. They can revisit this tool and look for progress.

TOOL 7.7 A PORTRAIT OF TRUST

This tool helps teachers imagine how their team will look and sound when members behave in ways that reflect trusting relationships. Use this tool after teachers complete Tools 7.6a and 7.6b.

- Be sure each teacher has a copy of the tool.
- Provide chart paper and markers.
- Ask teachers to work alone to identify some behaviors and attitudes that help people form trusting relationships and to write their ideas in the spaces provided on the handout.
- Ask team members or table groups to share ideas. Then invite them to construct a large portrait of trust on chart paper. Their portrait should identify attitudes and behaviors.
- Ask teams to post their charts, and have participants walk around and examine the trust portraits.

TOOL 7.8 TEAM COMMUNICATIONS

This tool helps teams understand the importance of logs and explains what information they should include.

- Be sure each team member has a copy of the tool.

- Ask teachers to scan the handout silently.
- Have chart paper and a marker available.
- Point out that learning team logs do not need a template. The idea is to capture the big ideas from team discussions and to record decisions so that others who read the log have richer information about the meeting.
- Explain that the log also acts as the next meeting's agenda. Teams should plan the next meeting during the current session, and the recorder should note that information in the log.
- Say that names, dates, and times should be included in every log.
- Lead a brainstorming session. At the top of the page of chart paper write: *How might your team logs be used?* Lead teachers in brainstorming ideas. (Tool 4.8 provides a protocol if needed.)
- Share information from the chapter background to provide additional ideas if needed. Point out that professional learning team logs typically are not used for accountability and are not meeting minutes.
- Invite participants to ask questions about the importance and use of team logs.

TOOL 7.9 ANYWHERE SCHOOL MEMO

Use this activity with Tool 7.10 to give teachers an example of nonproductive talk about an issue and experience with structuring productive conversations.

- Be sure all teachers have a copy of this memo.
- Ask teachers to read the memo and react to it in their teams or table groups. They should respond as if they were talking with colleagues in the teachers' lounge.
- Give teachers several minutes of talk time.
- Ask teachers to analyze the conversation they just had. Ask: 1) What facts did teachers share, if any? 2) What feelings did they share? 3) What decisions, if any, did they make?

- Invite them to discuss the memo again, then introduce Tool 7.10.

TOOL 7.10 HOLD PRODUCTIVE CONVERSATIONS

This tool can help gently structure conversations so that they begin with sharing facts and end with a decision.

- Be sure each teacher has a copy of the productive conversations handout.
- Explain that this conversation guide involves asking questions at four different levels numbered on the handout. Give teachers time to review the information.
- Suggest that team members discuss again the Anywhere School memo, this time using the productive conversations handout to guide their conversation.
- Allow time for the conversation, then ask teachers to talk about the differences in the two types of conversations they had and the value of the productive conversations process.
- Explain that this process also can guide team conversations into productive channels.

TOOL 7.11 CONVERSATION QUICK GUIDES

This tool can give teachers a quick guide for specific types of team discussions.

- Copy this tool on heavy paper, preferably card stock. Be sure each team or teacher has a copy.
- To prepare "flip strips," cut apart the Quick Guide cards and fasten them together at one end with a brad. Or ask a volunteer from each team to prepare the flip strips before the first team meeting.
- Explain that in meetings, team members will have a number of discussions as they share books and articles, plan teaching activities, and reflect on their progress. These guides contain questions

they can ask to focus their conversations. One guide offers instruction for developing questions to lead a conversation on any issue that arises not covered by the guide.

- Explain that when a team has an important matter to discuss, a conversation guide can help lead to a productive conversation and a decision.
- Let team members look through the conversation guides. Suggest they use the conversation guide, "Plan for the next meeting," to think through their next professional learning team meeting.
- Suggest the team keep a set of conversation quick guides in their notebook.

TOOL 7.12 UNDERSTANDING STUDENT THINKING VIDEO OBSERVATION GUIDE

This tool can help team members examine oral student responses or student performance tasks so they can make informed decisions about student thinking and learning. While it is written as a video guide, it also works well for examining student written work.

- Copy and distribute this guide when team members need help analyzing student work, including oral responses and performance tasks.
- Point out that team members do not need to answer every question, just those that will be useful in gaining the understanding they need.

TOOL 7.13 REGROUP BEFORE THE MEETING

This tool can help teams that are unhappy with the way their last meeting went and want to make changes in the current meeting.

- Be sure each teacher has a copy of the tool.
- Before the meeting, suggest that one team member lead this discussion to be sure the issues that sabotaged the last meeting are addressed and the meeting gets off to a positive start.

- If participants have the conversation quick guides available (Tool 7.11), call attention to a quick guide titled "Reflect on the meeting." This tool can help them think through the high and low points of the meeting.

TOOL 7.14 TEAM PROGRESS SELF-ASSESSMENT

This tool can help teams evaluate several aspects of team meetings, including interpersonal skills and activities. Teams often enjoy reviewing their ratings to gauge progress. This tool also reminds the team of good professional learning team practices and keeps these practices visible.

- Make sure each teacher has a copy of this tool.
- Suggest that teams use this tool once every four to five meetings to determine whether team members feel the team is operating well.
- Explain that each team member should respond to these descriptors by placing an "X" along each line to indicate where he or she thinks the team scores.
- Ask team members next to discuss their responses and fill out one chart as a team.
- Suggest that team members use the information to determine what areas of their team meetings are strongest and which need improvement.

TOOL 7.15 ARE WE ON TARGET?

This poster can help teachers focus on what they should accomplish through their team meetings.

- Prepare a copy of the poster for each team. You may make this larger and more attractive using a word processing program and larger paper. Laminate it if possible.
- Give each team a copy of the poster and ask them to place the poster in their meeting area.
- Ask teams to place a checkmark in the correct box for each descriptor after every third meet-ing. If the poster is laminated, suggest they use a water-based marker that they can wash off. If the poster is not laminated, make multiple copies for each team.

- Explain that if they are not "Doing great!" in an area, they should check the box on the left. Say that "Doing great!" means that all members are adhering to this indicator regularly and the action is now a normal part of the way the team does business.

CHAPTER 8

Maintain team momentum

This chapter will help the facilitator:
- Sustain teams as they continue their work;
- Establish and support effective communication; and
- Provide productive feedback.

"Successful change of individuals' knowledge and practices in classrooms and schools appears to be accompanied by ongoing support and assistance to them as they are implementing the changes."

— Shirley Hord,

Facilitative Leadership: The Imperative for Change,
1992

BACKGROUND

Getting one or more professional learning teams off the ground may seem like a Herculean task, but the most critical phase of the process is still ahead: building and sustaining momentum. Teachers generally are energized by workshops and other opportunities to gather for a professional purpose. They enjoy planning, preparing, and brainstorming together, especially when they're exploring new ideas they believe will help their students. Given this admirable teacher trait, learning teams likely will get off to a great start. But once teachers return to the day-to-day demands of school life, including the unanticipated demands on their time, their good intentions may take a back seat to the crisis of the moment.

Sustaining professional learning teams requires follow-up and support. When teachers participate in a professional learning team, they make a major commitment of time and energy. School leaders who provide ongoing encouragement, support, and resources for these professionals will be recognizing and honoring teachers' commitment and underscoring the importance of the teams' work to the entire school's success. Sustaining the work of professional learning teams is not a linear process, however. It requires continually revisiting, revising, and revamping support and facilitation.

TEAM DEVELOPMENT

Building productive teams takes time. Team members probably won't see immediate results. In fact, they should expect to be frustrated as they begin working together. Their learning team experience will take them through some predictable stages of development. To help teams gain and sustain momentum, help teachers recognize those stages and guide them through them.

> "These stages have major implications for professional development. First, they point out the importance of attending to where people are and addressing the questions they are asking when they are asking them. Often, we get to the how-to-do-it before addressing self-concerns. We want to focus on student learning before teachers are comfortable with the materials and strategies."
> — Susan Loucks-Horsley,
> *The Concerns-Based Adoption Model (CBAM): A Model for Change in Individuals,* 2005

Address teachers' stages of concern. Teachers' concerns about professional learning teams can strongly influence their team's performance. To help teams succeed, teachers must be able to understand and identify those concerns. The well-researched Concerns Based Adoption Model (CBAM) developed by Shirley Hord and Gene Hall (1987) outlines seven stages of concern (categorized under thoughts, feelings, and reactions) that people typically experience as they adopt an innovation. These concerns, adapted here for professional learning team work, are outlined in Tool 8.1. Notice that teachers move through these stages sequentially, progressing from concerns about the learning teams' effect on themselves, through concerns about how to best manage the teamwork, to concerns about the impact this initiative will have on others and how learning teams can be improved.

A second CBAM tool, Levels of Use, also can help teams determine their progress in implementing the professional learning team initiative. These levels describe people's behavior as they use an innovation, and more or less correspond to the Stages of Concern. Tool 8.2 applies the eight levels to professional learning teams. Combined information from the Stages of Concern and the Levels of Use can give teams an idea of where team members are in their development and use of professional learning teams. You can use this information to plan appropriate interventions and help teams move from one stage to another. Tools 8.1 and 8.2 include useful interventions for various stages of the team development process.

Understanding the Stages of Concern and the Levels of Use also can help you address that ever-present barrier — resistance. Resistance might surface, for example, because teachers don't have enough information about learning teams' work. They may be uncomfortable and stressed as they wonder, "What do I need to be able to do?" Understanding that their concerns likely stem from a lack of information can help you determine how to intervene and address that underlying anxiety that leads to resistance.

A deeper understanding of the Concerns-Based Adoption Model is valuable in planning, monitoring, and assessing a professional learning team's initiative. The National Staff Development Council online library (www.nsdc.org) provides many resources for understanding and using the Concerns-Based Adoption Model, as does the Southwest Educational Development Laboratory (www.sedl.org).

Address team interactions. Another way of examining team development is to observe team members' interactions as they work together. This process includes four often-cited stages of development that Bruce Tuckman (1965) identifies as forming, storming, norming, and performing.

1. In the *forming* stage, team members gener-

ally feel anticipation and optimism, coupled with some suspicion, uncertainty, and anxiety. The team may have difficulty getting a clear picture of its direction, and teachers may feel that they accomplish little, if anything, during these initial meetings. This is normal.

2. As teams continue meeting, they enter a difficult stage — *storming*. Team members realize the rigor of the work and the time and effort required. Teachers may be impatient, resistant, defensive, and argumentative. They may even question the wisdom of their collaboration. Often, team members cling to their current teaching experience and resist going deeper. This, too, is normal and may last for three or four meetings.

Getting off to a good start can help teams sustain their commitment during these early stages when the work seems to outweigh the benefits. To help them through these two stages, ask teams to prepare a chart with the meeting's purpose and what the team wants to accomplish during teachers' time together. Add the team goal to each meeting log to help everyone stay focused. To help teams stay on track with following their ground rules, pull out Tools 4.1, 4.6, and 4.7 from Chapter 4. Encourage teams and provide resources during these stages. Reassure them that their experience is a common one.

3. When team members begin to better understand the team's purpose and to put in place concrete steps to accomplish their goal, they enter the *norming* stage. Their enthusiasm returns, and teachers may even get off track because they are tempted to go beyond their original goal. Team members accept ground rules and roles, and a team spirit emerges. Relationships typically become increasingly harmonious and accepting.

4. In the *performing* stage, teams establish trust, and members accept one another's strengths and weaknesses. They perform as a cohesive unit

rather than as a collection of individuals. Team members work together and feel a collective sense of responsibility for the team's success. In this stage, teachers take concrete steps toward changing teaching practices and exploring more effective ways to instruct students. Students, too, generally begin showing signs of increased motivation and achievement.

In thinking about sustaining and supporting teamwork, keep in mind that both teachers and teams must progress through specific stages. Whatever stage they are in is OK, as long as they continue to progress after a reasonable period of time. Allow them to move through the stages at their own pace, and help when they are stuck.

Tools 8.3, 8.4, and 8.5 can help teams reflect on their development and work out plans to move forward.

PRODUCTIVE FEEDBACK

Feedback is another powerful strategy for sustaining teams. In fact, quality feedback can help teams improve, persevere, and become productive. Timely and regular feedback encourages team members by giving them an indication of their progress and keeping them focused on their purpose. Good feedback also confirms that you and other leaders are interested in the team's work and intend to help members develop and succeed. The school principal is especially critical in providing regular, constructive feedback.

Feedback can be face-to-face and written. For example, you may drop by team meetings to voice support for teachers' work. Respond regularly to team logs. Consider this scenario:

The team recorder keeps notes of the big ideas from the team meeting, the decisions the team makes, and plans for the next meeting. The recorder e-mails this log to the principal, other members of the team, and the entire staff. The principal reads the log and immediately sends a reply to everyone who received the log. As other faculty members read the log, some reply with questions or an "Atta-team!"

Think about this description. In less than five minutes, the principal read the log and sent feedback about teaching and learning to the whole staff. The log actually set up the principal to function as an instructional leader and gave her an opportunity to engage in a brief virtual conversation with all teachers. The principal's feedback also gave the learning team's work schoolwide recognition and indicated support for the professional learning team process.

The same quick and positive interaction can occur with logs posted on a web site such as a wiki or interactive web page. When logs and feedback are shared schoolwide, new opportunities for faculty engagement open up. Teachers across the school may become interested in other teams' work and respond to logs. Their feedback may help build stronger relationships and a sense of professional community.

Initially, teams may be reluctant to e-mail logs to the entire staff. Wait until teachers are comfortable with the team work before suggesting they share logs schoolwide. However, logs should be sent routinely to team members, the principal, and school leaders involved in providing feedback.

Feedback should be effective, constructive, and productive. Negative or disapproving feedback makes team members feel devalued and angry and will probably backfire. Effective feedback boosts team morale and teachers' self-confidence. It produces a "can-do" attitude that energizes teams. Follow these tips to provide the kind of feedback teams need.

TIPS FOR PROVIDING FEEDBACK

- **Be specific.** Tell teams — in detail — what you like about their work. Acknowledge particular issues and activities addressed in their log.
- **Provide feedback regularly and in a timely manner.** Provide immediate feedback, or tie feedback as closely to the team log as possible.
- **Focus on actions and events rather than on individuals.** Build trust and good relationships while providing useful support.
- **Keep all public feedback upbeat.** Use stems such as "This really made my day … ," "You're doing a great job with …" etc.
- **Share information, but not advice.** Have team members reflect on problems, not follow advice. Don't suggest what they should do. Instead, give them information they may need, and then ask questions that engage them in thinking, problem-solving, and building their own capacity to find solutions.
- **Don't overload team members with information.** Give teams the amount of information they need to address a specific issue rather than overwhelming them with all the resources at your disposal.
- **Feedback is more effective when team members request it.** If teams do not request feedback, or if they are not expecting feedback, then ask permission to provide feedback. Say, for example, "I'd like to give you some feedback about your meeting. Will that be OK?"
- **Use feedback to recognize and praise teams.** Recognition is powerful and motivating, and it generally leads to a repetition of the behaviors you praise.

When you must address specific problems with a team or redirect team members' efforts, talk privately. Team members will respond better to constructive feedback when your earlier feedback indicates that you have seen, heard, and understood them, and will work to support them as they change. Analyze the teams' perceptions of the feedback provided using Tool 8.6.

TEAM TUNE-UPS

Even the most enthusiastic teams need periodic checks to be sure they are operating efficiently, remaining purposeful, and moving steadily toward their objective. Members may need to revisit the team's goals and learning plan, rethink their norms, and possibly do some troubleshooting. To help keep teams moving steadily forward and growing, frequently revisit school support structures and professional incentives.

Revisit your school support structures. A supportive school culture provides the backdrop for successful teams. Re-examine the school supports suggested in Chapter 3, then consider:

- *Teacher roles.* What roles are teachers playing in the school? Does the school organization reflect the belief that teachers are professionals and that instruction is their most important job? Or are teachers required to perform clerical, bookkeeping, and managerial tasks? Be sure that what teachers are asked to do day-to-day gives them time and energy to plan for and provide quality instruction. Make whatever changes are needed to allow teachers to focus on what really counts.

- *Risk taking.* Teachers must be willing to take risks with new instructional strategies and must know they have the school leader's permission to do so. Provide "risk-free teaming." Actively encourage teachers to experiment, learn from mistakes, and develop their full potential. Tools 8.7 and 8.8 can ease risk-taking anxiety by giving teachers (and facilitators) permission to try new things, even if they are not immediately successful. Remind teachers that they will not learn as much from what goes well as they will learn from what does not. With that perspective, lack of success is not frustrating or embarrassing but an opportunity to learn.

- *Celebrations.* Is the school celebrating professional learning team activities and successes? Spotlight teacher and student activities that are outgrowths of professional learning team work. Post announcements in the teacher workroom, in school newspapers, and in office areas where parents can see the teams' progress. Schedule a time for learning teams to share their successes during faculty meetings. Occasionally provide refreshments for team meetings. Give each team a surprise basket of office supplies and food. Tool 8.9 offers another suggestion. Also, ask teachers to offer ideas for how they would like to celebrate their team learning.

You might arrange for groups outside the school to recognize learning teams' work. Invite the local paper to write an article, or ask businesses to provide assistance or materials for teams. Be sure to publicly support all teams during the school year.

- *Priorities.* Are team meetings given a high priority at the school — both for teachers and school leaders? Unless attendance and active involvement are priorities, teams' written goals will never come alive for teachers or their students. Some team members begin professional learning team work because they passionately believe that teachers — those closest to the students — should be the ones to solve teaching and learning problems. They are correct, but the path to success leads directly through the meeting room door.

> **"The goal is to feel safe enough to indulge in risk taking. Leaders should not try to prevent mistakes but should stress that they are to be welcomed, examined, and understood as natural phenomena — as a necessary part of learning."**
> — Nancy Mohr & Alan Dichter, *Phi Delta Kappan*, 2001

One way to emphasize that professional learning teams are a schoolwide priority is to protect teams meeting times. Use bulletin boards or other areas in the school office and the faculty workroom to post team schedules and announcements. Take pictures of teams working, and post these as well. Sustain teams' momentum by emphasizing that office personnel, other teachers, and students should honor each team's meeting time and avoid interrupting. Use Tool 8.10 to help.

Revisit professional incentives. People learn to behave certain ways through the rewards or negative consequences that follow their behavior. Recognizing and rewarding a behavior increases the likelihood that staff will repeat that behavior, and the action may eventually become part of the school culture.

Once learning teams are under way, watch for additional ways to thank teachers for putting extra time and effort into upgrading their skills, changing teaching practices, increasing knowledge, and better preparing students. Even a simple thank you from the school principal for work well-done can help shape the culture of the school.

Revisit the incentives outlined in Chapter 3 and decide if any of the suggestions here will provide additional ideas for ways to sustain teachers' work.

- *Connect professional learning team work with other school programs and initiatives.* Make professional learning teams a central, ingrained part of the school's commitment to improved teaching and learning. For example, connect professional learning teams' work to the school improvement plan and to individual teacher professional growth plans. Connecting the initiatives teachers are expected to implement helps them maintain their enthusiasm and energy for participating in professional learning teams.
- *Offer education credit for professional learning team work.* Arrange for continuing education credit through the local college or university, or through the central office. Learning teams can easily document their professional development activities using meeting logs, team plans, and portfolios.
- *Regularly showcase teams' work.* Spend time sharing work results at faculty meetings by eliminating general announcements, school management issues, and negativity. Make sharing by one or more learning teams a regular item at the top of the agenda to give instructional issues their proper importance. School leaders who use faculty meeting time this way send a message about their priorities.
- *Give team members opportunities and training on using technology to communicate and promote their work.* E-mail, electronic logs, web-based newsletters, and other tools can spread the word and promote the potential of technology to support professional development in general. A technology coordinator might set up an area on the school web site where teams can post announcements, best ideas and practices. Blogs, wikis (easy-to-use, interactive web pages), and other types of collaborative networking technology can engage all teams and the wider community in ongoing exchanges of ideas and information.
- *Create a learning team identity.* Even something as simple as designing a professional logo to use on team communiqués conveys the important message that there's nothing ordinary about these teams.

HUMAN RESOURCES

Teams need to be "resource rich" if they are to sustain momentum. How do team members access research and information to continue learning and growing professionally? Tool 8.11 lists ideas.

Among these ideas, colleagues are a valuable and often untapped resource for information and insight. Consider this excerpt from an Alabama elementary school professional learning team log. Team members gathered ideas for furthering their math questioning skills by visiting other classrooms.

"We found it extremely valuable to be able to see the growth in thinking and questioning as we traveled from kindergarten to 5th grade. We also were grateful to be able to step outside our own grade levels to observe older/younger students as they shared their strategies."

— *A Hoover, Ala., elementary school teacher*

Providing substitutes and allowing team members to spend a day using their colleagues as resources paid real dividends. Not only did team members gain new and valuable insights, they built stronger relationships and gained new respect for one another.

When classroom observations are not feasible, teams may videotape one another. For example, teaching assistants in one North Carolina school met regularly as a learning team to study strategies for incorporating reading into other content areas. At each meeting, they studied a reading comprehension strategy that they then practiced and videotaped in the classroom during the week. At meetings, they shared clips from their videotapes and critiqued the strategy. Videotaping enabled them to become peer mentors and coaches for one another.

Tools 8.12, 8.13, and 8.14 can help faculties share expertise.

PROGRESS CHECKS

Regular team self-assessments are crucial for keeping teams focused and moving in the right direction. Self-assessment tools keep a best-case scenario on team members' radar. As team members gauge their progress, they also consider what ideal progress might look like and focus on where they need to go. Comparing a team assessment with the same assess-

ment taken earlier in the year can also energize teams as they see evidence of progress. Tool 8.15 can help.

Facilitators, too, need to do periodic self-assessments. Ask teams to use Tool 8.16 or a similar method to provide feedback on what you are doing well and what additional help team members would like. Use the information to revamp and refine support for the teams.

Asking team members for feedback can be daunting, especially if the teams are not running smoothly or are resistant to implementing a new initiative. If a person (or team) makes unhelpful or negative comments, take a "balcony" position — look at the comments impersonally and from a psychological distance. Don't regard any comments a team member makes as "good" or "bad." Regard them all as "interesting" and ask, "What do I need to do with respect to this feedback?"

The information and tools in Chapter 8 and other chapters can help focus energy on keeping professional learning teams moving forward. Change is difficult, and progress is sometimes inconsistent; nevertheless, with persistence, teams can reach their goals. The outcome is worth the effort.

Chapter 8 facilitation guide

The tools for this chapter help facilitators keep professional learning teams motivated and moving. Each tool contains an explanation and a suggested method of using that tool with groups of teachers. Decide whether you need to use a particular tool and adapt it if necessary based on the needs of the teachers you work with.

TOOL 8.1 STAGES OF CONCERN ABOUT PROFESSIONAL LEARNING TEAMS

This tool can help individual team members consider their previous and current reactions to the professional learning team initiative and be aware that they will move from one level of concern to another as the initiative progresses. This tool also is designed to help the facilitator determine appropriate assistance and interventions to provide to team members when they get stuck in a stage.

- Copy this tool and distribute it to each team member.
- Share information from the chapter background section to introduce the Concerns-Based Adoption Model. Lead teachers to understand the stages of concern shown on this tool.
- Invite teachers to reflect on each stage and how they might feel and think at each level (columns 1 and 2). Ask them to decide where they are along this continuum. Suggest they place a check mark beside each stage of concern through which they think they have progressed.
- When team members reach a stage they don't feel they have worked through, invite them to share what they are feeling and thinking about professional learning teams. Make notes of personal concerns members are experiencing.
- Explain that the third column contains ideas you suggest to build comfort levels and gradually

TOOLS

move individuals to the next stage.
- Use the information from the discussion plus your own observations to help you understand teachers' concerns and sticking points.

TOOL 8.2 LEVELS OF USE

Use this tool to help team members understand that teams, like individuals, go through different levels as they work toward quality implementation of an initiative. Also use this tool to gather information that can help you provide appropriate intervention when teams are stuck at one level. Team members should understand that where they are is OK, but they do not want to remain at any level indefinitely. Point out that each team works through these stages over time and at its own pace.
- Make copies of this tool and distribute it to each team member.
- Share information from the chapter background

section on stages of team development to introduce teachers to the Concerns-Based Adoption Model. Guide them in becoming familiar with the eight levels of use.

- Ask team members to identify behaviors in the second column that they have already experienced. For example, do they feel they have passed through the nonuse stage?
- Suggest that team members determine at what level their actions and experiences appear to be clustering now.
- Explain that the third column contains activities and assistance that might keep them moving past each stage until they reach renewal.
- Lead team members to discuss with you ways that they can use this information. Remind them that where they are now is a good place to be, and now they know that they will eventually move through other levels.
- Use the information from this activity, along with your own observations, to plan for your work with the teams. What needs to happen to move them toward the next stage of development?

TOOL 8.3 TOOL TALK

Use this tool to have team members describe the team's work so far, sharing their hopes and expectations for future meetings, and considering any changes needed to maintain their momentum.

- Prepare copies of this handout for each teacher. Also provide chart paper and markers.
- Invite teachers to examine the tools depicted on the handout and choose a tool that they think represents, in some way, their team's work. Explain that they may choose a tool not pictured.
- Ask team members to discuss their selections and explain why they picked that tool to represent their team's work. Recommend that a volunteer list on chart paper the characteristics of the

team's work that teachers identify.

- When team members complete the activity, invite them to examine the chart and add any information.
- Instruct the recorder to write "Team Portrait" at the top of the chart.
- Suggest that teachers reflect on the picture portrayed by the information on the chart and decide what parts of that picture they want to keep and what they want to discard. For each part they decide to discard, ask them to suggest a specific way to remove that behavior from their team.

TOOL 8.4 ASK THE RIGHT QUESTIONS

This tool can provide a problem-solving approach for team members to use when the team seems stuck.

- Make a copy of this tool for each team member. Explain that this tool can help jump-start the team when it seems stuck.
- Ask each teacher to silently reflect and list three or more questions that need to be asked about the team's progress. Suggest they focus on questions to which the team can work out answers and solutions.
- Tell team members to share their questions. As each question is shared, ask, "Did anyone else have that question?" Suggest that team members not repeat the same questions as they share.
- Chart questions that team members think need to be answered for their team to move forward. Then call attention to the questions one at a time and ask:
  - How will knowing the answer to this question help the team move forward?
  - What are some possible answers to this question?
  - What are our next steps with regard to this question?

- As teams identify next steps, make a to-do list on a different sheet of chart paper. Ask team members to decide on responsibilities.

TOOL 8.5 THE BALCONY VIEW

This tool provides a safe way for teachers to talk about the work of their team and team relationships. Ideally, this activity allows team members to take an outside position and look more objectively at the team's work and to understand how they might better function within the team.

- Provide a copy of this tool for all teachers, along with chart paper and markers.
- Ask each teacher to imagine that he or she is on a balcony watching the professional learning team in operation. Ask each to describe what she or he sees. Ask each to answer:
  1. Where is the team meeting?
  2. Who is present?
  3. How are team members seated?
  4. What are they doing?
  5. What are they saying?
  6. What specific attitudes and behaviors do you observe?
- When all team members have written responses, ask them to share their view of the meeting they observed. You may want a volunteer to chart some items that seem to give an accurate picture of the team.
- Invite team members to stay on the imagined balcony, but to put themselves into the team meeting. Ask, "What are you doing that is making a difference for your team?" Suggest that team members think in terms of what they ideally would be doing, and ask them to list their imagined actions and behaviors on the handout.
- Ask for volunteers to share the behavior they identified, but do not pressure teachers to share. The value of this part of the activity is in devel-

oping awareness of how individuals' behaviors influence the team.

- Ask team members to suggest the worth of this activity. This kind of visualizing may help them develop a clearer picture of their team's functioning and a greater awareness of how they can influence that functioning.

Variation: To break up the tedium of handouts, you might cut 8½ x 11 sheets of paper into strips lengthwise. Post sheets of chart paper on the wall. Rather than ask teachers to write their balcony observations on the handout, ask them to write each behavior they visualize on a different paper strip. Direct them to tape these strips to chart paper and to group similar responses together. To debrief, ask them what behaviors and actions they agree paint a correct picture of their team. Teachers should write their individual reflections about the team roles they play on their handout to maintain their privacy unless they wish to share.

TOOL 8.6 FEEDBACK ANALYSIS

This tool lets team members express their perceptions about the quality and usefulness of feedback they have received. It also gives facilitators a checklist to remind them what feedback should look and sound like.

- Make copies of this tool for each team member.
- Give team members the option of filling out this tool individually (and anonymously) or as a team.
- Collect the forms and analyze the responses.
- Provide copies of the responses to everyone who has provided feedback to teams.
- Select one or two areas for improving feedback, and begin to work on these immediately. Add areas as manageable.
- Do frequent checks with teams to see whether they think feedback is improving.

TOOL 8.7 IT'S OK! CARDS—TEACHER VERSION

Use this tool to give teachers permission to take a risk, fail, and try again. Remind them that we do not learn as much from our successes as from our failures. Not succeeding can motivate us and offer us an opportunity to learn.

- Copy and cut apart the cards. Give each team member a card.

- Explain that changing the way we teach is difficult and requires trial and error. Although teachers will use research-based strategies, instruction will not always go smoothly. You want teachers to feel free to take risks. This ticket gives them permission to try a new strategy, fail, and try again. It also entitles them to support from you and their colleagues.

- If teachers express dismay because a teaching approach did not get the desired results, use this opportunity to distribute the "It's OK!" cards again. Keep reminding them teaching and learning is always a work in progress. And that's OK!

TOOL 8.8 IT'S OK! CARDS—FACILITATOR VERSION

This tool, similar to Tool 8.7, reminds facilitators that getting professional learning teams up and running, and keeping them running smoothly, is a demanding task that will have ups and downs. Facilitators are taking the lead against a long-standing culture of isolation. Expect fits and starts. Expect things not to work smoothly, and know that that's OK. Team members and facilitators alike can use lack of success as an energizer to keep pushing forward.

- Copy and cut apart the cards. If you are working with other facilitators, give each one a card. Keep a stack for yourself, and help yourself to them as needed! Then regroup, revise, shake off any dejection, and keep going!

TOOL 8.9 SOMETHING TO CELEBRATE

This tool can remind teams and the school staff of an upbeat way to create and sustain team momentum. Use this procedure to help teachers and other school staff remain positive and focused on their progress. This tool works well as a wall chart and can be used to spotlight individual teams or all teams collectively.

- Give a copy of this tool to each team and suggest that the team keep a running list of accomplishments. Members can write one item in each area of the patchwork quilt.

- When a team fills up the quilt's spaces, suggest they turn this quilt into a wall poster and place it where others can see.

- You may wish to prepare a large, collective patchwork quilt poster for the entire faculty that spotlights the good things happening schoolwide through professional learning teams. Be sure to include blank spaces for teams to continue adding accomplishments as the year goes on. You may also want to wait until teams submit a list of accomplishments to you before preparing this poster so that it doesn't appear empty of successes.

TOOL 8.10 PROTECT THESE TEAMS!

This poster can help remind office personnel and others to guard team meeting times from interruptions. Write your team meeting day and time on the poster. Put the poster on the office bulletin board or in a designated area.

- Prepare multiple copies of this poster on card stock paper. If team meeting times do not change, the same schedule can remain posted. When meeting times change, post a new schedule. Consider enlarging this poster, laminating it, and providing dry-erase markers so that teams can make changes to the posted meeting times as needed.

- Ask each team to write its meeting day and time

on the poster. Put the poster on the office bulletin board or in a designated area.

- If you made one large poster and laminated it, place dry-erase markers near the poster, and ask teams to write their meeting times on the poster. Post this in a prominent place where office staff, students, and other teachers will see it.

- Copies of this form can also be placed near team meeting areas to remind others that teachers are collaborating and must not be interrupted.

TOOL 8.11 FINDING RELEVANT RESOURCES

Using a variety of resources can give teachers multiple perspectives and ideas. This tool is an information resource for teachers.

- Copy and distribute this tool to all teachers.

- Suggest that team members read each suggestion and decide on at least three new sources of information to use.

- Teachers may have questions about some of the web resources described. Explore these resources yourself, and add to the list as you discover new tools for virtual information sharing. Also contact technology experts. Students can be good assistants in searching out appropriate web tools and information for team members.

TOOL 8.12 DATABASE OF TEACHER TALENT

This tool can help you systematically gather information about the talents and skills of teachers in your school (or beyond). Use the information you gather to determine what knowledge and expertise your faculty can share with one another.

- Provide a copy of this tool to every teacher.

- Ask teachers to fill out the requested information. Explain that teachers will not be compared, but the information will help identify specific expertise, teaching strategies, and interests so faculty members know whom to call on if they need a

consultant or peer coach in a particular area.

- Collect the information. If the school is technologically capable, ask a volunteer to create a database and post it to the web, or organize the information so it's easily accessible by everyone.

TOOL 8.13 HUNTING FOR HELP

Teams can use this tool to enlist colleagues' help in sharing specific knowledge and skills.

- Make several copies of this tool for each team.

- Explain that as teams look for resources and information on specific topics and instructional strategies, they may wish to call on faculty for help. These forms can help them locate those willing to assist.

- Suggest they fill in the appropriate information, duplicate the form, and place the forms in teachers' boxes or in the teacher workroom.

- If a faculty member volunteers to help, recommend that the team write a special thank-you card or that members offer another gesture of appreciation.

TOOL 8.14 SHARE A SITE

This tool lets faculty share useful web sites they have identified.

- Provide a copy of this tool to every teacher.

- Ask teachers to list sites directly related to topics that professional learning teams in the school are addressing or sites that display lesson plans and other relevant online resources.

- Arrange for teachers to return this form to you at a designated time.

- If the school is technologically able, ask a designated person to use this information to build a database of online resources for your faculty.

TOOL 8.15 TEAM PROGRESS REMINDERS

This tool can help teams take ownership of their

progress by examining progress indicators and developing their own rating scale to monitor improvement.

- Distribute two hole-punched copies of this tool to each team. (You might also give a copy to individual team members as a reference while the team reaches consensus on the questions.)
- Tell team members that it's time to check their progress. Ask them to review and discuss these 10 questions to help them identify their current success level.
- Invite team members to make up their own rating scale to assess how close they are to giving a question a thumbs-up. Remind them that wherever they are is OK, as long as they are progressing.
- Suggest that team members reach consensus on where they think their team currently ranks on each question, and place this copy of the progress check in their team notebook. They could include a second copy of the tool in the notebook to use later and compare the two to determine progress.

TOOL 8.16 FACILITATION CHECK

This tool provides a way to gather ideas and input from team members on support they are receiving and would like to receive.

- You might use one of two approaches:
  1. Meet with team members briefly and gather oral feedback. (Keep this short if done during regular team meeting time.) In that case, you will need one copy of the form on which to record the ideas they offer.
  2. Distribute a copy of this form to each team member and ask each person to anonymously fill it out and place it in a predetermined location. Then compile their ideas and answers for each question.

- Use the information you gather to reflect, revamp, and refine your support for the teams. If a person (or team) makes unhelpful comments, go to that mental balcony. Look at comments impersonally and from a distance, not as "good" or "bad." Regard them all as "interesting," and ask yourself, "What do I need to do based on this feedback?"

EXAMINE RESULTS

CHAPTER 9

Assess team progress

This chapter will help the facilitator:

- Assess the impact of professional learning teams on teacher growth and development;
- Provide teams with additional tools for formative self-assessments;
- Determine if the professional learning team process is changing classroom instruction; and
- Gather data for making decisions about next steps for professional learning teams.

"A good evaluation system requires that evaluators collect substantive formative data to use to tweak a program, keep it on track, or get it back on track. Adjusting any program as it progresses is essential to getting positive long-term results."

— Robby Champion, *JSD,* 2005

BACKGROUND

When schools devote significant time, energy, and resources to an initiative such as professional learning teams, then district leaders, the community, and those in charge of resources want to see evidence of the value. In addition, team members want data to guide their work, and they will be motivated to continue in the effort by seeing outward signs of success. So how will you systematically establish whether professional learning teams are improving results for students, teachers, and the school as an organization?

External evaluations can provide objective and useful information to justify the continued need for the learning team initiative to school boards or other agencies. Internal evaluations are valuable for making informed decisions about midcourse adjustments and actively involving teachers in examining the results of their work throughout the process.

The process of guiding a school to collaboratively develop its own internal evaluation for professional learning teams is beyond the scope of this book, but *Assessing Impact: Evaluating Staff Development,* by Joellen Killion (Corwin Press and NSDC, 2008), can guide you in developing an evaluation. The process Killion describes is well worth investing the time, effort, and energy. However, you can use the tools in this chapter to gather informative data without having developed a more comprehensive evaluation procedure.

TYPES OF INFORMATION TO GATHER

Many teams begin a new professional learning

initiative enthusiastically, then drift into old patterns and eventually crumble. If you plan the evaluation process early and use a variety of tools to routinely monitor team progress and develop interventions, setbacks are less likely. Begin by thinking about what should happen as learning team members work together throughout the year. They should grow in their ability to work together smoothly as a team, become more knowledgeable and effective in their work, and have a positive impact on school morale and student learning. How can you systematically determine whether these things are happening?

Donald Kirkpatrick, author of *Evaluating Training Programs: The Four Levels* (Berrett-Koehler, 1998), suggests using four levels of evaluation to assess new initiatives or programs:

- Level 1: Reaction. How did participants react to the program training?
- Level 2: Learning. How did participants' attitudes, knowledge, and skills change as a result of the program?
- Level 3: Behavior. What changes in participants' behaviors occurred as a result of the program?
- Level 4: Results. What results were achieved because of the program?

As you apply Kirkpatrick's model to professional learning team training and work, keep team members actively involved by sharing results of surveys, questionnaires, and other data-collection procedures with them, or let them analyze the data and share the results with you. The data will provide a basis for adjusting the

> **Administer team surveys online**
> Consider putting some surveys online in an easy-to-use format through a free online survey service. If your system does not provide an online survey tool, type "online surveys" into an Internet search engine to locate free online survey services.

learning team process to ensure continuing progress. Some types of data to collect are:

1. Teacher reactions.

How did teachers react to the initial training? After introducing professional learning teams to teachers, survey teachers for their reactions to this initiative. Were they confused? Was information missing? Were teachers engaged? Do they see new possibilities for improving their teaching?

At the end of the introductory session, give teachers a questionnaire that measures their degree of satisfaction with the training and asks them to evaluate the experience. If they feel good about the initial experience, they will be more supportive of the learning team process in the important early stages. Tool 9.1 includes questions and a rating scale to use to gather information about teachers' reactions.

2. Teacher learning.

What are teachers learning as they work together in professional learning teams? What teachers learn as they work in teams will influence their beliefs, attitudes, and thinking about collaborating with colleagues. Collect data that focus on teachers' beliefs and attitudes about learning teams, and track how their thinking changes over time. Use Tools 9.2 and 9.3 to collect baseline data on teacher thinking and beliefs about learning teams. Use the same tools quarterly to compare team members' attitudes and beliefs at different stages of their learning work.

To determine whether teachers are learning more about collaboration and teaching, examine team meeting activities. Are team members reflecting on ways to improve their teamwork? Are they reading and discussing research-based materials? Sharing craft knowledge and skills? Reflecting on strategies to improve student learning? Some of this information will be documented in team logs, and other data can be collected through informal observations. Use Tools 9.4 through 9.8 to gather information on what teachers are learning about teaming and teaching.

3. Teacher behaviors.

How have teachers applied their learning to their interpersonal interactions and teamwork? Teachers' traditional patterns and habits of interaction should change after working in learning teams. Are teachers meeting more regularly in teams to learn, becoming more interdependent as team members, basing instructional decisions on research, observing other teachers, developing new instructional materials, and building stronger professional relationships?

Team logs, focus groups, retrospective surveys, samples of collaboratively developed materials, and informal observations are good ways to gather evidence. You can use Tools 7.14, 8.15, 9.7, and 9.8 to determine how team members' interactions and relationships are changing as a result of working in learning teams.

How are teachers applying what they learn to their classrooms? Gather evidence that teachers are transferring new knowledge and skills from professional learning teams to actual classroom practice. Teachers might be using new instructional methods, assessing the impact of new teaching strategies, adjusting instruction based on assessment findings, and perhaps videotaping their teaching for their team to view and analyze. Team logs, classroom observations, focus groups, and/or retrospective surveys are good sources of data for monitoring classroom applications. You can use Tools 9.4 through 9.8 to gather this data.

4. Results.

What results are professional learning teams achieving for students? Teachers might look for evidence of changes in student engagement, motivation, and learning. Some teams meet to design classroom

CLASSROOM SNAPSHOTS

The learning team facilitator at Cranford Burns Middle School in Mobile, Ala., and faculty members decided to use walk-throughs to see how school instructional strategies changed over time. At the beginning of the initiative, the facilitator collected baseline data about what instructional strategies teachers were using by conducting 10-minute observations across all classrooms. The facilitator did not record information about specific teachers, and the survey was not used for evaluation. Later in the school year, the facilitator took another set of classroom snapshots. Teachers then compared the results to determine whether and how classroom instructional practices were changing.

assessments, including performance assessments, that help them measure the impact of their work on student learning. Photographs and videos of students working in classrooms can help document changes. Additional sources of information include samples of student work and norm- and criterion-referenced tests. When looking at student standardized test scores for evidence of success, however, be cautious before attributing increased test scores to the impact of the learning team process. Claiming a direct link requires a strong research design that controls for other variables that also might affect standardized scores.

What changes in school morale and culture are occurring in conjunction with professional learning teams? Strong and productive learning teams typically create changes in school morale and culture. Although other factors also contribute to culture change, schools in which adults collaborate for professional learning seem to go hand-in-hand with school cultures in which adults and students trust and care for each other and draw energy from one another (Strahan, 2003). Tools 7.6a and 7.6b can help teachers track changes in trust levels among team members and could be used with the whole faculty. You can also use observations, team logs, and perceptual surveys, such as Tool 9.2 and Tool 9.3, to track changes in teacher attitudes and beliefs.

Artifacts such as copies of faculty meeting agendas also might reflect changes growing out of the learning team process. For example, one learning team facilitator tracked the amount of time the staff spent in faculty meetings discussing instructional issues. In August, the meetings included almost no time dedicated to instruction. As professional learning teams took root, the amount of faculty meeting time devoted to instructional issues rose steadily. By January, traditional administrative matters moved to the bottom of the list as teachers demonstrated new teaching practices and discussed their learning teams' progress. By the end of the year, nearly all of faculty meeting time focused on classroom instruction. Data of how time is used, along with other information, can support the conclusion that professional learning teams affected the school culture.

Robert Garmston and Bruce Wellman's *The Adaptive School: A Sourcebook for Developing Collaborative Groups* (Christopher-Gordon, 1999) contains an excellent team self-assessment (pp. 292-295), along with other tools to evaluate group development.

OTHER CONSIDERATIONS

If possible, arrange for an outside evaluation midway through the year and again at the end of the year. Evaluators could be consultants, college professors, or business people who understand teamwork, education, and learning communities. Ask evaluators to conduct structured focus groups with individual learning teams to determine what changes are occurring as a result of the learning team process and to collect teacher reflections on the process. Share and discuss the results with team members. Together, use this information to rethink the project's direction and facilitation.

As you continue throughout this collaborative process, look for any new resources that will help you assess the effectiveness of professional learning teams and help team members gauge their progress so learning teams can improve results for students, teachers, and the school organization.

Chapter 9 facilitation guide

The tools for this chapter include data-collection methods that facilitators and team members may use throughout the project to collect information about team progress and results. Each tool contains an explanation and a suggested method for using that tool. Some tools should be used at regular intervals — perhaps quarterly — during the professional learning team process to help teams assess themselves and stay on track.

TOOL 9.1 PARTICIPANT PERCEPTION SURVEY

Use this questionnaire to determine teachers' reactions after you present information on professional learning teams. Give teachers a questionnaire at the end of the introductory session to measure their degree of satisfaction with the training, and ask them to evaluate the experience.

- Copy the questionnaire and provide a copy to each participant.
- Allow 10 minutes at the end of the workshop or presentation for teachers to record their perceptions. Distribute the questionnaires at that time.
- Explain that the questionnaires should be anonymous. Instruct teachers to check the box that most closely approximates their perception of each item. Clarify that the highest rating is 5 and the lowest rating is 1.
- Tell teachers what to do with the questionnaires when they finish. You might ask them to place the questionnaires face down on a table near the door as they leave.

TOOL 9.2 PRE/POST SURVEY

This tool provides baseline data from teachers who will participate in the learning team process. It can give you a quick overview of where to focus training and support. The survey also could be of-

TOOLS

9.1 Participant perception survey

9.2 Pre/post survey

9.3 Survey of teacher beliefs about teaming

9.4 Year one debriefing questions

9.5 Year two planning questions

9.6 Checkpoint survey

9.7 Our team members

9.8 Professional learning team survey

fered online through a free online survey service.

- Make a copy of this questionnaire for each teacher or put the questionnaire online. If you put it online, be sure to use a survey form to which teachers can respond anonymously and set a deadline for responses.
- Assure teachers when you hand out a copy that the survey is anonymous.
- Distribute the survey to teachers before they begin the professional learning team process and at the end of the first school year of implementation. Also give the survey periodically throughout the year to track how teachers' knowledge, attitudes, and actions are changing.
- Compare responses to determine what changes are occurring in teachers' reactions to and beliefs about professional learning teams.

TOOL 9.3 SURVEY OF TEACHER BELIEFS ABOUT TEAMING

This tool provides baseline data on what teachers think and believe about professional learning teams before you introduce the initiative to the faculty. Use the results of this survey, along with information from Tools 8.1 and 8.2, to identify teachers' concerns and motivation, and then decide what information and tools to use to begin to build learning teams. Administer the survey at the end of each semester, and compare the results to gauge any changes in teachers' perceptions and attitudes about learning teams. Share results with team members so that they, too, can see changes.

- Make a copy of this survey for each teacher or put the survey online. If you put it online, be sure to use a survey form to which teachers can respond anonymously and set a deadline for responses.

- Distribute the survey before introducing the professional learning team initiative. Make sure teachers know the survey is anonymous. Emphasize that there are no good or bad responses and that all answers will be respected and valued.

- Explain that you will use teachers' current perceptions about working together in teams to help you decide where to start when introducing the initiative. Tell teachers that you will give them the survey again at the end of each semester in order to track changes in teacher perceptions. Assure them that you will share each set of results with them.

- After you have collected the surveys, analyze the data and decide which attitudes and beliefs you will address through training, support, and incentives. Prepare a slide or handout to use in sharing anonymous survey responses with teachers. Do not share a response that might embarrass or easily identify a teacher.

This survey may be turned into a rating-scale survey by adding ratings beneath each question rather than leaving the question open-ended. One value of rating scale surveys is that participants' responses are easy to tally. The disadvantage is that the responses you collect may not be as diverse, rich, or informative.

TOOL 9.4 YEAR ONE DEBRIEFING QUESTIONS

Use this tool to debrief teams at the end of the first year of the process. Gather information from teams or individual members, or from a representative sample of participating teachers. Change, omit, or add questions as needed.

- Meet with each team, or with a representative sample of learning team participants from the faculty.

- Explain that you need honest feedback in order to adjust and improve the professional learning team process.

- Ask the questions and record team members' responses. Do not comment except to ask for clarification. Remind team members to follow team norms for responding, with no one person dominating and with everyone participating.

- As an alternative, copy this form and distribute it to teams, asking for written responses, or put the survey online. If you put it online, be sure to use a survey form to which teachers can respond anonymously and set a deadline for responses.

TOOL 9.5 YEAR TWO PLANNING QUESTIONS

This tool provides a reflective questionnaire that can encourage teams to assess their work from the previous year and set a direction for work in the coming year. While the title refers to year two, this tool can be used at the beginning of any year.

- At the beginning of the school year, copy the tool for each team member or put the survey online. If you put it online, be sure to use a survey form to which teachers can respond anonymously and set a deadline for responses.

- Invite team members to share and discuss their responses for each question.

- Ask team members to give you a copy of their responses if they feel comfortable doing so. Explain that the answers to the last four questions in particular will help you plan guidance and assistance.

TOOL 9.6 CHECKPOINT SURVEY

Team members can use this tool to periodically check their team's functioning and to select areas for greater improvement. The survey statements represent a best-case scenario and can remind teams what they can achieve.

- Distribute a copy of this tool to each team member, and prepare an extra copy for each team.
- Ask team members to individually rate each statement in terms of how well it applies to their professional learning team meetings.
- Ask team members to compile their answers and average the totals. They should mark the averages on the extra team survey form, then include it in their notebook for reference and comparison.
- Tell teams to look at their lowest ratings and decide how they can begin to improve in these areas. Recommend that they select no more than two areas.
- In the event that team members rank each item "agree" or "strongly agree," suggest they look at those marked "agree" and begin to push toward the highest rating. If a team ranks every item as "strongly agree," suggest they select one or two areas for additional emphasis.

TOOL 9.7 OUR TEAM MEMBERS

This tool lists ideal attributes of team members. It can help team members periodically assess individuals' growth and participation, select areas for improvement, and remind them what an ideal scenario would look like. The group can fill it out as a whole, or team members can use it as an individual assessment.

- Distribute a copy of this tool to each team member and an extra copy to each team.
- Ask team members to place a check mark beside each statement they believe describes their team and to list at least one bit of evidence that supports this belief.

- Suggest that team members compare their answers and evidence, then reach consensus on which statements they feel accurately describe their team. They should place a check mark by these statements on the team survey form and file it in their notebook for reference and comparison.
- Invite teams to examine the statements with no check marks by them and to decide how they can improve in these areas. Recommend they select no more than three areas for improvement at a time.
- If team members feel that all statements describe their team, suggest they select one or two areas for additional emphasis.

TOOL 9.8 PROFESSIONAL LEARNING TEAM SURVEY

This survey gathers a variety of information on professional learning teams and teachers' perceptions of them.

- Make a copy of this survey for each participant at the end of the school year.
- Tally results, carefully disaggregating information to draw accurate conclusions about a learning team's value.
- Managing this survey may be easier online with a service that automatically tallies teachers' responses as they complete the survey.

FACILITATE THE PROCESS

CHAPTER 10

Lead for success

This chapter will help the facilitator:

- Learn some tips for good facilitation;
- Discover ideas for ways to encourage and support teams; and
- Gain some tools for working with school leaders.

"Preparing today's students to participate in a global, knowledge-based economy is a demanding challenge. No teacher should be expected to do this job alone. It is time to give educators the support they need to succeed. For decades, we have been managing school improvement with command-and-control, regulatory, prescriptive, or market-based incentives that treat school leaders, teachers, and students like the targets of change rather than the agents of change. We need to replace these approaches with strategies that empower those individuals to lead and shape the reinvention of their own learning organizations."

— The National Commission on Teaching and America's Future, 2007

BACKGROUND

The word *facilitate* means *to make easy*. The facilitator's job is to make the professional learning team process as smooth and productive as possible for teachers. Teachers already are shouldering increasing responsibilities, workloads, and expectations. Assist them with learning team logistics. Help them acquire resources. Be their advocate and run interference. Protect their meeting times from outside interruptions. Foster the attitude throughout the school that greater student success may hinge on the teacher learning and development that occurs in these team meetings.

Facilitators also need to develop skills to work effectively with teams. These 10 tips may help you move the professional learning team process smoothly forward.

1. Be resilient. Keep a sense of humor, and remain objective during the ups and downs that are a natural part of any process. Never take teachers' frustrations with the professional learning team process personally. Bolster their morale and focus on helping teams deal with frustrations. You and team members are learners together in this process.

2. Be flexible and responsive. Change is seldom

smooth. Be alert to possible mid-course corrections that need your intervention. Above all, be transparent and willing to admit mistakes while staying grounded in the basics of the professional learning team process.

3. Be an encourager and a motivator. An upbeat, friendly, and thoughtful attitude will aid the team's progress. Help team members deal with the daily distractions that make it difficult for even the most motivated to protect their meetings from interruptions. Gently nudge teams who seem to be returning to their old habits. Provide frequent feedback and show interest in what teams are accomplishing. Share success stories with the entire faculty to help everyone see that what teachers are learning and doing in professional learning teams is making a difference for students.

4. Promote and reinforce team members' beliefs in the benefits of working together and in their ability to work together productively. Be aware of team members' levels of motivation and commitment, and be ready to intervene when these wane. For example, give professional learning teams high visibility schoolwide and point out what teams are accomplishing. Provide continuous feedback to teams and promote communication among teams. Invite teachers to give written testimonials that can be shared with other faculty members. Keep a list of each team's accomplishments, and pull out this information when teams start to doubt their effectiveness.

When teachers become complacent or unenthusiastic, help them focus clearly on the purpose of their professional learning team work and the results it should produce. Try to reestablish a sense of purpose. Create short-term wins for teachers by celebrating successes and benchmarks achieved.

5. Build rapport with teams. Team members are more likely to go the extra mile if they trust and respect you. Build strong relationships with team members, and hidden agendas and resentments are less likely to cloud success. Use informal processes to build good relationships with team members, such as showing respect, appreciating and celebrating their achievements, and staying in regular contact. Tool 10.3 offers additional ideas for building rapport.

6. Draw up a contract. At the beginning of the learning team process, work out with teachers what the facilitator will do with and for the learning team and what team members will be responsible for. Tool 10.4 provides an example of a contract between the facilitator and a team. Discuss this idea with teachers after they understand the purpose and procedures of professional learning teams. Put agreed-upon decisions and responsibilities in writing, and distribute copies to learning teams to make decisions more concrete.

7. Continue to read and learn about professional learning teams. Throughout your role as a facilitator, study and reflect. Acquire a good working knowledge of the role professional learning teams

AN ATMOSPHERE OF COMMUNITY

"My professional learning team creates an atmosphere of community within a very busy environment. It brings people together to share ideas and methodologies to strengthen student learning and minimize teacher burnout. I've enjoyed the process because it forces me to think outside of my comfort zone and it pulls my colleagues together on the same page."

— *Edna Lawrence,*
D.F. Walker Elementary School, Edenton, N.C.

play in improving teacher expertise and student learning. This guidebook tries to distill some of the best current thinking about professional learning teams, but most facilitators will want to look beyond these pages. The references section points to books and articles that can provide you with a growing knowledge base about collaborative professional learning.

8. Gather evidence of results. Regularly gather data (team logs, observed changes in classroom practices, surveys, etc.) to track and document progress. Keep an eye out for results: What positive changes are occurring as a result of this process? What evidence demonstrates these changes? What is not happening that should be happening? Share evidence and data regularly with teams and others who are interested. Tool 10.5 can help facilitators spotlight growth.

9. Fine-tune those presentation skills. A facilitator sometimes assumes the role of a trainer, helping teachers learn to become successful team members. An excellent resource on thoughtful, purposeful, and powerful presenting is Robert Garmston's *The Presenter's Fieldbook: A Practical Guide*, (Christopher-Gordon, 2005). Another resource is a book by Karen Kalish: *How to Give a Terrific Presentation,* (AMACOM, 1997). Both are included in the references list.

While a discussion of presentation skills is beyond the scope of this book, keep these points in mind.

- When making a presentation to teachers, choose the time and place carefully. Teachers' energy levels often lag at the end of the school day, and many find it difficult to concentrate in after-school faculty meetings. Put the professional learning team work first on the agenda, or better yet, make team learning the only thing on the agenda.
- Keep the presentation short, upbeat, and to the

point. Design any slide presentation to enhance learning. Garmston's *The Presenter's Fieldbook: A Practical Guide* has a section, "PowerPoint Tips and Traps," that can help.

- During and after the presentation, build in time for faculty members to process information, question, reflect, and discuss. This is the most important part of any presentation, as this is the point at which teachers begin to internalize and make sense of the information presented.
- When making a presentation to or sharing information with school leaders, include information from Tools 10.6 to 10.11 to clarify the characteristics of successful professional learning teams, encourage reflection about school policies that help or hinder teams' success, and highlight the importance of effective leadership.

> **"The brain can only absorb what the seat can endure."**
> — Karen Kalish, *How to Give a Terrific Presentation,* 1997

10. Expect resistance. The issue of resistance has been mentioned in previous chapters, but bears mentioning once more. Resistance to change seems to be a built-in characteristic of schools and school systems. Monica Janas (1998) describes resistance as "the sleeping dragon of the change process" that "thwarts goals, disrupts action plans, and undermines progress." Don't be surprised or disconcerted when this sleeping dragon rears its head. Refer to Tools 7.5, 7.6, 7.7, and 10.3 for help in defusing resistance by building good personal relationships with and among team members.

The most formidable opponent of professional learning teams is the status quo. Teachers are part of that status quo. Remember that change of any kind is complex and difficult. The decision to create professional learning teams may have been accompanied initially by a glow of rosy optimism. However, as in any change process, predictable conflicts and difficulties occur as the project progresses. Expect these, and deal with them objectively. Document the pitfalls as well as the successes, and learn from both. Tool 10.11 helps team members reach consensus on important team decisions.

A FINAL WORD OF ADVICE

Do not try to persuade teachers to participate in learning teams by assuring them the change will be easy. Principals and teachers should acknowledge from the outset that changing their teaching practice will be difficult, regardless of how carefully they plan and how skillfully they manage the process. They must understand the magnitude and scope of the change. Above all, remember that each team is unique, and each school situation is unique. Groups mature at different rates, and some will perform better than others.

As you build a school culture committed to higher levels of learning for both students and faculty, remember that the journey is seldom easy or without mishaps along the way. But the learning opportunities afforded and the ultimate reward in renewed enthusiasm, cooperation, and improvement will be worth the effort.

And as you facilitate these new professional learning teams, you, too, will experience aha moments and insights and will create your own tools for assisting teams. Share those tools and discoveries with others engaged in this same journey. Your personal learning and experiences will provide additional insights about professional learning teams and add to the growing body of knowledge of ways to revolutionize 21st-century teaching and learning.

Chapter 10 facilitation guide

These tools are designed primarily for facilitators. Some provide tips for facilitating professional learning teams, and others may be used with principals and administrators. Select the tools most suited to your needs and purposes, and adapt the suggestions as needed for your purposes and situation.

TOOL 10.1 THE FACILITATOR'S ROLE

This tool reviews some of the responsibilities of a professional learning team facilitator. The list is not comprehensive and may be adapted as needed.

- Use this list to create a job description for a professional learning team facilitator. A job description might help in gaining funding for a position.

- Use the tool as a checklist. Select several concrete tasks to accomplish.

- Use this list to generate ideas for competencies you can gain as the process continues.

TOOL 10.2 ORGANIZE FOR THE JOURNEY

Good facilitation begins with organization. Documenting each team's history and progress is crucial. This tool can give you ideas for information and artifacts you need to track throughout the process.

- Collect information from the first day on. File a copy of anything prepared, sent, or done to facilitate the professional learning team process.

- Decide how to keep up with the information. Will you organize the data electronically, on paper, or both? Set up a procedure before beginning the professional learning team work.

TOOL 10.3 BUILD RAPPORT WITH TEAMS

Trusting relationships are critical to creating effective teams. Good facilitators know their team members and deliberately nurture positive connec-

TOOLS

tions. This tool offers tips for behaviors and actions that build good rapport with team members.

- Think objectively about each team and its members. How well do you know them? What type of relationships do you have with them?

- Read through the relationship-building behaviors. A list of ideas appears beneath each category, but add your own ideas in the spaces beneath the bullets.

- Beside each behavior category is room for you to reflect on what you are doing or have done in that area. Your notes may serve as a reminder and as a checklist for intentionally building good relationships with teams.

TOOL 10.4 A SAMPLE PROFESSIONAL LEARNING TEAM AGREEMENT

This tool provides a sample agreement between a facilitator and members of professional learning teams.

- First allow the team to organize and determine the team goal.

- Work with professional learning team members on an agreement to clarify both your role and the expectations for team members.

- Make copies of this tool, if needed, to jump-start team members' thinking, or draw up a sample agreement of your own for teachers to examine.
- Be sure that both the facilitator and each team get a copy of the completed agreement.

TOOL 10.5 INFORMATION CHECKLIST FOR FACILITATORS

As teams proceed with their work, use this tool to track where they are in the process. Keep in mind that some benchmarks, such as applying new instructional strategies, will not happen initially. Use this checklist to get snapshots of a team over time, to note changes, and to gain ideas for where you might intervene to help teams progress.

- Make several copies of this checklist for use with each team you facilitate.
- After visiting a team meeting, periodically complete this checklist to get a quick picture of the team's behaviors and activities. Keep in mind that one visit is not an accurate picture; however, completing several checklists over time may indicate some team strengths and weaknesses.
- Use this checklist to share with teams areas in which you observe growth and to ask questions about areas you did not observe.
- Don't use this tool for accountability or to cause teams to feel they are being judged.
- Keep in mind that some activities (such as applying new instructional strategies) may not happen until later in the process.

TOOL 10.6 PROFESSIONAL LEARNING TEAMS THAT WORK

This tool highlights characteristics of schools that have produced successful professional learning teams and seen positive changes in classroom instruction and student learning.

- Make copies of this tool for each principal or leader.
- Explain that this tool outlines characteristics of professional learning teams in schools that have experienced positive changes in teaching and learning using this approach.
- Help administrators and teachers understand the scope of the undertaking, as well as potential outcomes.
- Invite them to consider which characteristics are present in their own schools and to identify steps to put in place desired characteristics.

TOOL 10.7 IS THIS A GOOD POLICY?

Some school policies can actually sabotage professional learning teams. This tool allows school leaders to analyze existing policies, programs, or procedures and make adjustments that can smooth the way for successful collaboration.

- Prepare copies for each participant. Include teachers, principals, and other leaders.
- Invite participants from the same school to sit together, if applicable. If not, have participants sit in groups of three or four.
- With other school leaders, use these questions to discuss specific policies and procedures in place at your school. Include both written policies and traditional ways of working that are firmly in place. For example, in some schools, administrators highly structure teachers' meeting times.
- Invite participants to decide on a policy that seems to need the most attention in terms of advancing teacher collaboration and professional learning.
- For each policy discussed, invite each person to place an X along the continuum beneath each question to indicate what he or she thinks about the policy under consideration. Then ask the group to discuss members' perceptions of the

policy. If the policy does not help build a collaborative school culture with shared leadership and vision, discuss how to begin making needed policy changes.

- For more information about policies that support professional learning teams, read "Policies that support professional development in an era of reform," by Linda Darling-Hammond and Milbrey W. McLaughlin (1995).

TOOL 10.8 HOW IMPORTANT ARE YOU?

This tool can help school leaders understand the impact of leadership on both teacher achievement and student achievement and the importance of the role they play in professional learning teams. Prepare a copy of this tool for each principal or school leader.

- Suggest they read the first three statements silently. Then ask them to discuss these questions: "What, if anything surprised you?" "Which of these findings makes you feel most hopeful?"

- Ask participants to look at the ideas for successful professional learning team leadership. Explain that these ideas are adapted from a 2004 study, *How Leadership Influences Student Learning*, by the Wallace Foundation. Suggest they discuss these findings with others at their table. Then use Tool 4.8 to brainstorm a list of ways school leaders might accomplish these three actions. Ask a volunteer to chart the information.

- List actions you will take to successfully lead the professional learning team.

TOOL 10.9 WHAT'S A LEADER TO DO?

This tool gives an overview of actions principals can take to support professional learning teams.

- Prepare a copy for each principal.
- Prepare for each group of principals a set of numbers, 1 through 15. Cut the numbers apart.

- Invite principals to shuffle the numbers and place them face down on the table. Ask them to take turns drawing a number and matching it with a number on their handout. Give them a choice of explaining how they would accomplish that action, or allow them to call on another participant to respond.

TOOL 10.10 SAMPLE NOTE FROM AN ADMINISTRATOR

Communication and feedback from school leaders shows team members that leaders value their work and believe that professional learning is important. This sample note can give principals and administrators ideas for providing concrete direction and support to teams as they begin the professional learning team process. The note should be tailored to the needs of the school or district. Use it as an example of ways that you and other leaders might provide guidance, visibility, and a sense of importance to learning team work.

- Prepare and distribute a copy to each principal or leader.

- Explain that this message was sent by Barbara Howard, executive director of professional development for the Scotland County School System in North Carolina, to high schools in her district. This is an example of the type of message an administrator or principal could send to show initial support and provide direction as teams begin the process.

- Explain that this is not a note to copy, but several features in this note might be included in an initial message sent to teams in their district or school.

- Invite leaders to read the letter and identify features they think are worth emulating. They might see that the note provides teams with specific, concrete instructions and reiterates some features of professional learning teams that teams sometimes find difficult, such as an instructional focus. It also mentions specific support the central office will provide during the course of the work.

TOOL 10.11 CONSENSUS-BUILDING TIPS

Members need to feel ownership of and commitment to team decisions, such as setting the goal. If the full team does not support an important decision, you should attend a team meeting and guide members in reaching consensus on that issue. Consensus involves looking for a decision or solution that is acceptable to all team members and helping team members who did not agree with the team's decision find some level of commitment. This tool features questions to guide team members toward consensus.

- Read the information on Tool 10.11 and list questions you will ask team members.

- Have chart paper and markers available.

- At the meeting, assure team members that your purpose is to see that everyone's concerns are heard, understood, and respected by the whole team.

- Set guidelines for the discussion. Explain that team members should:
  - Express ideas and thinking openly.
  - Listen carefully to what others have to say.
  - Be open to and respectful of others' experience, opinions, and thinking.
  - Actively seek agreement and look for common ground.
  - Be flexible and willing to give up some positions in order to reach an agreement.
  - Ask the questions you listed and invite all team members to respond to each question. Draw out responses from those who oppose if they do not initially respond. Chart the responses so that everyone can keep track.

- When everyone has responded, ask the group to suggest a solution that might be acceptable to all members. Write this decision on the chart paper.

- Ask for a show of agreement. Explain that team members may:
  - Agree ("I support the decision as written").
  - Disagree ("I do not support the decision as written").
  - Agree with reservations ("I can live with the decision as written").

- If any team members object, refine the proposal.

- If team members are unable to reach consensus, ask a subgroup to develop a proposal, taking into account the concerns discussed, and bring it back to the next meeting.

References

Barkley, S. (1999, Fall). Time: It's made, not found. *Journal of Staff Development 20*(4), 37-39. Oxford, OH: NSDC.

Beatty, C. & Scott, B. (2004). *Building smart teams: A roadmap to high performance.* Thousand Oaks, CA: Sage Publications.

Bolam, R., McMahon, A., Stoll, L., Thomas, S., & Wallace, M. (2005). *Creating and sustaining effective professional learning communities* (Department for Education and Skills Research Report RR637). Available at www.dfes.gov.uk/rsgateway/DB/RRP/u013543/index.shtml.

Brosnan, M. (2003, Winter). At the heart of the heart of the matter: Interview with Roland S. Barth. *Independent School Magazine, 62*(2).

Bryk, A.S. & Schneider, B.L. (2002). *Trust in schools: A core resource for improvement.* New York: Russell Sage Foundation.

Caudron, S. (2000). Keeping team conflict alive. *Public Management, 82*(2), 5-9.

Champion, R. (2005). Identify the payoffs for investment in better program evaluation. *JSD, 26*(3), 62-63.

Covey, S. (1997). *The 7 habits of highly effective families.* New York: Golden Books.

Darling-Hammond, L. (1995). Policy for restructuring. In Ann Lieberman (Ed.), *The work of restructuring schools: Building from the ground up.* New York: Teachers College Press.

Darling-Hammond, L. (1999, Spring). Target time toward teachers. *Journal of Staff Development, 20*(2), 31-36.

Darling-Hammond, L. (2000, January 1). Teacher quality and student achievement: A review of state policy evidence. *Education Policy Analysis Archives, 8*(1). Available at http://epaa.asu.edu/epaa/v8n1/.

Darling-Hammond, L. & McLaughlin, M.W. (1995, April). Policies that support professional development in an era of reform. *Phi Delta Kappan, 76*(8), 597-604.

Delisio, E. (2006). Principal unites school around student strengths. *Education World School Issues.* Available at www.education-world.com/a_issues/chat/chat180.shtml.

DuFour, R. (2004, Summer). Leading edge: Are you looking out the window or in a mirror? *JSD, 23*(3), 63-64.

DuFour, R., Dufour, R., Eaker, R., & Karhanek, G. (2004). *Whatever it takes: How professional learning communities respond when kids don't learn.* Bloomington, IN: Solution Tree.

DuFour, R. & Eaker, R. (1998). *Professional learning communities at work: Best practices for enhancing student achievement.* Bloomington, IN: Solution Tree.

Ferguson, R. (1999, December 9). Testimony given in CFE v. State of New York. Available at www.cfequity.org/Fergus.html.

Fullan, M. (1993). *Change forces: Probing the depths of educational reform.* London: Falmer Press.

Fulton, K., Yoon, I., & Lee, C. (2005, August). *Induction into learning communities.* Washington, DC: National Commission on Teaching and America's Future.

Gable, R. & Manning, M. (1999, January 1). Interdisciplinary teams: Solution to instructing heterogeneous groups of students. *The Clearing House, 72*(3), 182-185.

Garmston, R.J. (2005). *The presenter's fieldbook: A practical guide* (2nd ed.). Norwood, MA: Christopher-Gordon.

Garmston, R.J. & Wellman, B. (1999). *The adaptive school: A sourcebook for developing collaborative groups.* Norwood, MA: Christopher-Gordon.

George, J. & Wilson, J. (1997). *Team member's survival guide.* New York: McGraw-Hill.

Gideon, B. (2002, October). Structuring schools for teacher collaboration. *Education Digest, 68*(2), 30.

Hall, G. & Hord, S. (2005). *Implementing change: Patterns, principles, and potholes* (2nd ed.). Boston: Allyn & Bacon.

Hanushek, E.A. (2002). Teacher quality. In L.T. Izumi & W.M. Evers (Eds.), *Teacher Quality* (pp. 1-13). Stanford, CA: Hoover Institution Press.

Hanushek, E.A., Kain, J.F., O'Brien, D.M., & Rivkin, S.G. (2005, February). *The market for teacher quality* (NBER Working Paper No. W11154). Available at http://ssrn.com/abstract=669453.

Hord, S. (1997). *Professional learning communities: Communities of continuous inquiry and improvement.* Austin, TX: Southwest Educational Development Laboratory.

Inger, M. (1993, December). Teacher collaboration in secondary schools. *Center Focus, 2.* Available at http://ncrve.berkeley.edu/CenterFocus/CF2.html.

Janas, M. (1998, Summer). Shhhhhh, the dragon is asleep and its name is Resistance. *Journal of Staff Development, 19*(3), 13-16.

Jolly, A. (1998). *Anne's action research diary.* Available at www.middleweb.com/mw/images/jollydiary.pdf.

Kalish, K. (1997). *How to give a terrific presentation.* New York: Amacon.

Killion, J. (1998). Learning depends on teacher knowledge. *Results.* Available at www.nsdc.org/library/publications/results/res12-98killion.cfm.

Killion, J. (2008). *Assessing impact: Evaluating staff development* (2nd ed.). Thousand Oaks, CA: Corwin Press and NSDC.

Kirkpatrick, D. (1998). *Evaluating training programs: The four levels* (2nd ed.). San Francisco: Berrett-Koehler.

Langer, J. (2001, Winter). Beating the odds: Teaching middle and high school students to read and write well. *American Educational Research*

Journal, 38(4), 837- 880.

Lewis, L., Parsad, B., Carey, N., Bartfai, N., Farris, E., Smerdon, B., Greene, B. (1999). *Teacher quality: A report on the preparation and qualifications of public school teachers.* Washington, DC: National Center for Education Statistics.

Leithwood, K., Louis, K.S., Anderson, S., & Walhstrom, K. (2004). *How leadership influences student learning: Review of research.* Minneapolis, MN: Center for Applied Research and Educational Improvement and Toronto, ON: Ontario Institute for Studies in Education.

Lewis, L. (2001). *Teacher preparation and professional development: 2000.* Washington, DC: U.S. Department of Education, National Center for Education Statistics. Available at http://nces.ed.gov/surveys/frss/publications/2001088/.

Lieberman, A. & Miller, L. (2000). Teaching and teacher development: A new synthesis for a new century. In *Education in a new era: 2000 ASCD yearbook.* Alexandria, VA: ASCD.

Little, J.W. (1990). The persistence of privacy: Autonomy and initiative in teachers' professional relations. *Teachers College Record, 91*(4), 509-537.

Loucks-Horsley, S. (2005). *The Concerns-Based Adoption Model (CBAM): A model for change in individuals.* Washington: National Academy of Sciences. Available at www.nas.edu/rise/backg4a.htm.

McHugh, J. (2005, October). Synching up with the iKid. *Edutopia.* Available at www.edutopia.org/ikid-digital-learner.

Mistretta, R.M. (2005). Mathematics instructional design: Observations from the field. *The Teacher Educator, 41*(1), 16-33.

Mohr, N. & Dichter, A. (2001). Building a learning organization. *Phi Delta Kappan, 82*(10).

Murphy, C. (1997, Summer). Finding time for faculties to study together. *Journal of Staff Development, 18*(3).

Murphy, C. (1999, Spring). Use time for faculty study. *Journal of Staff Development, 20*(2).

Murphy, C. & Lick, D. (1998). *Whole-faculty study groups: A powerful way to change schools and enhance learning.* Thousand Oaks, CA: Corwin Press.

National Center for Education Statistics. (2005). *Characteristics of public school teachers' professional development activities: 1999-2000.* Washington, DC: Author. Available at http://nces.ed.gov/pubsearch/pubsinfo.asp?pubid=2005030.

National Commission on Teaching and America's Future. (1996). *What matters most: Teaching for America's future.* New York: Author.

National Commission on Teaching and America's Future. (2007, October 24). *Pledge to organize schools for success.* Available at www.nctaf.org/resources/events/PledgetoOrganizeSchoolsforSuccess.htm.

National Education Commission on Time and Learning. (1994). *Prisoners of time.* Washington, DC: Author.

National Staff Development Council. (2001). *NSDC's standards for staff development.* Oxford, OH: Author.

Nussbaum-Beach, S. (2008). 21st Century Collaborative blog. Available at http://21stcenturylearning.typepad.com/.

O'Connell, J. (2005). A message from the superintendent. *Middle Grades Spotlight.* Available at www.cde.ca.gov/re/pn/nl/documents/mgnewsltrsum05.doc.

Pruet, S. & Duke, J. (2007). *Understanding Student Thinking (USE) protocol.* Mobile, AL: Mobile Math Initiative.

Raths, J. (2001). Teachers beliefs and teaching beliefs, *Early Childhood Research and Practice, 3*(1). Available online at http://ecrp.uiuc.edu/v3n1/raths.html.

Richardson, J. (1997, October/November).

Honoring all voices crucial in consensus. *Tools for Schools,* 8.

Richardson, J. (1999, August/September). Norms put the 'golden rule' into practice for groups. *Tools for Schools.*

Richardson, J. (2002, August/September). Think outside the clock: Create time for professional learning. *Tools for Schools,* 1-2.

Rossett, A. (1999). *First things fast: A handbook for performance analysis.* San Francisco, CA: Jossey-Bass.

Sanders, W. & Rivers, J.U. (1996). *Cumulative and residual effects of teachers on future student academic achievement.* Knoxville, TN: University of Tennessee Value-Added Research and Assessment Center. Available at www.heartland.org/Article. cfm?artId=3048.

Stanfield, R.B. (Ed.). (2000). *The art of focused conversation: 100 ways to access group wisdom in the workplace.* Gabriola Island, British Columbia, Canada: New Society Publishers.

Stigler, J. & Hiebert, J. (1999). *The teaching gap: Best ideas from the world's teachers for improving education in the classroom.* New York: The Free Press.

Strahan, D. (2003, November). Promoting a collaborative professional culture in three elementary schools that have beaten the odds. *The Elementary School Journal, 104*(2), 127-146.

Trimble, S.B. & Peterson, G.W. (2000). *Multiple team structures and student learning in a high-risk middle school.* Paper presented at the annual meeting of the American Educational Research Association, New Orleans, LA.

Tuckman, B.W. (1965). Developmental sequence in small groups. *Psychological Bulletin, 63*(6), 384-399.

U.S. Department of Education. (2000). *A talented, dedicated, and well-prepared teacher in every classroom.* Washington DC: Author. Available at www.eric.ed.gov/ERICDocs/data/ericdocs2sql/content_storage_01/0000019b/80/16/5b/c0.pdf.

Van Slyke, E. (1997). Facilitating productive conflict. *HR Focus, 74*(4), 1.

Von Frank, V. (Ed.). (2008). *Finding time for professional learning.* Oxford, OH: NSDC.

Wald, P. & Castleberry, M. (2000). *Educators as learners: Creating a professional learning community in your school.* Alexandria, VA: ASCD.

Wright, S.P., Horn, S.P., & Sanders, W.L. (1997). Teacher and classroom context effects on student achievement: Implications for teacher evaluation. *Journal of Personnel Evaluation in Education, 11*(1), 57-63.

Resources

"A measure of concern: Research-based program aids innovation by addressing teacher concerns," by Karel Holloway. (2003, February/March). *Tools for Schools*.

"CBAM brings order to the tornado of change," by Donald Horsley and Susan Loucks-Horsley. (1998, Fall). *Journal of Staff Development, 19*(4).

"Data-driven schools," by John Norton. (2002). *Working Toward Excellence, 2*(3).

Facilitative Leadership: The Imperative for Change, by Shirley Hord. (1992). Available at www.sedl.org/change/facilitate/leaders.html.

How Teaching Matters: Bringing the Classroom Back Into Discussions of Teacher Quality, by Harold Wenglinsky. Princeton, NJ: Educational Testing Service, 2000.

"Learning teams: When teachers work together, knowledge and rapport grow," by Joan Richardson. (2001, August/September). *Tools for Schools*.

Moving Staff Development Standards Into Practice: Innovation Configurations, Vol. I, by Shirley Hord and Pat Roy. Oxford, OH: NSDC, 2003.

On Common Ground: The Power of Professional Learning Communities, by Richard DuFour, Robert Eaker, and Rebecca DuFour. Bloomington, IN: Solution Tree, 2005.

"Strengthening teacher quality in high-need schools policy and practice," by the Council of Chief State School Officers. (2007). Available at www.ccsso.org/publications/details.cfm?PublicationID=354.

Taking Charge of Change, by Shirley Hord, William Rutherford, Leslie Huling-Austin, and Gene Hall. Alexandria, VA: ASCD, 1987.

"Taking measure: Innovation Configurations gauge the progress of a new initiative," by Joan Richardson. (2004, October/November). *Tools for Schools*.

"Teachers' learning communities: Catalyst for change or a new infrastructure for the status quo?" by Diane Wood. (2007). *Teachers College Record, 109*(3), 699-739.

"Teacher learning that supports student learning," by Linda Darling-Hammond. (1998, February). *Education Leadership, 55*(5), 6-11.

Team Building: Developing a Productive Team, by Arnold Bateman. (1990). Available at http://ianrpubs.unl.edu/misc/cc352.htm.

Transformational Leadership: Using Quality Improvement Processes to Build a Learning Organization, by Ruth Ash and Maurice Persall. Unpublished manuscript. Birmingham, AL: Samford University, 1997.

"What is a 'professional learning community'?" by Richard DuFour. (2004, May). *Educational Leadership, 61*(8), 6-11.

"What does 'The world is flat' mean for public education?" by Chris O'Neil. (2006, October 17). *Edutopia*. Available at www.edutopia.org/what-does-world-flat-mean-education.

TOOLS

Tool 1.1: What do *I* know? What do *we* know?

Directions: You and a team of colleagues are helping to design a professional learning initiative for teachers in your school. The principal has promised you the resources you need to engage in effective professional learning.

Begin by considering three questions. Answer the questions individually, then form groups of three to four and share your answers. Make notes of any new ideas and information you gain as you share.

1.   What outcomes should result from a strong professional learning initiative?

_____

_____

_____

2.   What characteristics of quality professional learning should be included in this initiative?

_____

_____

_____

3.   What supports will teachers need in order to effectively participate in this professional learning?

_____

_____

_____

REFLECT: What value did working with a group add when answering these questions?

_____

_____

_____

REFLECT: What might be the value of regularly working with a group of teachers to improve instructional practices?

_____

_____

_____

Tool 1.2: Think about your professional learning

Directions: How does the professional learning you normally receive measure up? These statements describe some benefits of quality professional learning. Circle the answer that best describes to what degree you feel this description is true of the professional learning you participate in.

1. Fits naturally with our school system or school goals.
    Strongly disagree   *Disagree*   *Agree*   *Strongly agree*

2. Provides a consistent focus and ongoing training and assistance.
    Strongly disagree   *Disagree*   *Agree*   *Strongly agree*

3. Engages teachers in using multiple sources of data and information to determine student learning needs.
    Strongly disagree   *Disagree*   *Agree*   *Strongly agree*

4. Creates a collective commitment among teachers to deepen their content knowledge and to learn and use research-based instructional practices to meet student needs.
    Strongly disagree   *Disagree*   *Agree*   *Strongly agree*

5. Provides time and opportunities for groups of teachers to meet regularly to share, reflect, and work together on the art of teaching.
    Strongly disagree   *Disagree*   *Agree*   *Strongly agree*

6. Empowers teachers to make decisions about their own professional learning needs.
    Strongly disagree   *Disagree*   *Agree*   *Strongly agree*

7. Is relevant and useful to situations teachers face each day in the classroom.
    Strongly disagree   *Disagree*   *Agree*   *Strongly agree*

8. Provides a way for teachers to learn and grow in a supportive atmosphere.
    Strongly disagree   *Disagree*   *Agree*   *Strongly agree*

9. Honors teachers' current knowledge and skills.
    Strongly disagree   *Disagree*   *Agree*   *Strongly agree*

10. Provides teachers with a process for successfully dealing with individual student learning needs.
    Strongly disagree   *Disagree*   *Agree*   *Strongly agree*

11. Provides teachers with continuing opportunities to grow professionally at the school site and routinely integrate their learning into classroom practice.
    Strongly disagree   *Disagree*   *Agree*   *Strongly agree*

12. Engages teachers in spending greater amounts of time in professional learning.
    Strongly disagree   *Disagree*   *Agree*   *Strongly agree*

 REFLECT: Which of these professional learning characteristics are needed by teachers in your school?

_____

Tool 1.3: Look at teacher needs

DIRECTIONS: Think about your school as you read the statements below. Place a check mark next to the statements you think describe the needs of teachers at your school. Discuss the items you check with other participants nearby and explain your thinking.

_____ 1. We need to increase student achievement.

_____ 2. We need to continually increase our knowledge and teaching expertise.

_____ 3. We need to strengthen professional relationships, become less isolated from one another in our work, and create bonds of trust and caring.

_____ 4. We need to examine new ideas, implement new teaching strategies, and evaluate the impact on student learning.

_____ 5. We need to sustain changes in our teaching practices over the long term.

_____ 6. We need to effectively mentor and assist new teachers.

_____ 7. We need flexible, relevant, job-embedded professional learning.

_____ 8. We need to increase our teacher leadership capacity and skills.

_____ 9. We need to be regarded as valuable professionals and instructional decision makers.

_____ 10. We need a cost-effective way for all faculty members to engage in ongoing professional learning.

_____ 11. We need a practical way to implement new instructional initiatives.

_____ 12. We need a realistic way to engage in action research.

REFLECT: How could systematically working together in teams help us meet these needs?

_____

_____

_____

Tool 1.4: Will collaboration work?

Directions: Duplicate and cut apart the cards. Each team will receive one card, and then brainstorm ideas. Refer to Tool 4.8 for help brainstorming. Chart the team's ideas.

PROFESSIONAL DESIGN TEAM

You are members of Design Inc., a professional think tank that specializes in creating opportunities for professionals to engage in on-the-job collaboration and increase their skills and productivity.

Your firm has been hired by Innovation High School to develop an organizational structure, working conditions, and a procedure that will enable teachers to work together in teams to increase their knowledge and skills so that they become cutting-edge teachers. What will you recommend? What information, opportunities, and working conditions will teachers need to be able to work together effectively?

Brainstorm ideas and jot your plans on the chart paper.

Your design team has 10 minutes.

PROFESSIONAL SABOTAGE TEAM

You are members of Sabotage Inc., a firm that specializes in undermining attempts that would allow professionals to collaborate on the job and increase their skills and productivity.

Your firm has been hired to undermine a plan by Innovation High School. This school plans to create conditions that allow teachers to meet and work together to continually increase their knowledge and skills so that they are cutting-edge teachers.

Your job is to sabotage this plan. Design an organizational structure, working conditions, and procedures that will result in teachers working in isolation and will make it difficult for them to collaborate.

Brainstorm ideas and jot down your plans on the chart paper.

Your sabotage team has 10 minutes.

Tool 1.5: Quick quiz

Directions: Take this quiz and discuss your thinking with a small group of participants. You can find the answers in Tool 1.7, "What does the research say?"

1. **The most important determinant of student achievement is:**
   a. Socioeconomic status
   b. Teacher knowledge and expertise
   c. Parental and societal factors

2. **Most of the achievement gap between poor minority children and students in more affluent communities can be explained by:**
   a. Access to more resources and better facilities
   b. Family income and parental education levels
   c. Differences in the quality of teaching

3. **How much time per year does the average teacher spend in professional learning?**
   a. 8 hours or less
   b. 3 days
   c. One week

4. **What percent of teachers identified strong results from those learning experiences?**
   a. 8%
   b. 15%
   c. 42%

5. **Which group reported spending the least amount of time working together with colleagues on instruction?**
   a. Beginning teachers
   b. Elementary teachers
   c. Secondary teachers

6. **Teacher experience (years of teaching) is correlated with gains in teaching quality in what way?**
   a. The more experienced the teacher, the higher the quality of the teaching.
   b. There is no correlation between teacher experience and teaching quality.
   c. There is little or no correlation between experience and teaching quality after the first year of teaching.

7. **Which of these structures has proven to be essential for improving teaching quality?**
   a. Collaboration to improve instruction
   b. Supportive school conditions and culture
   c. Both A and B

Tool 1.6: Focus questions

Directions: Copy and place these tent cards on tables. Use these questions with Tool 1.7 to discuss the need for and benefits of professional collaboration.

QUESTION 1

Why do we need to continually improve
and adapt our instruction?

QUESTION 1

Why do we need to continually improve
and adapt our instruction?

QUESTION 2

Why should we work in professional learning teams to do this?

QUESTION 2

Why should we work in professional learning teams to do this?

QUESTION 3

How can working together on instruction make a difference for us?

QUESTION 3

How can working together on instruction make a difference for us?

QUESTION 4

How can working together on instruction make a difference for our students?

QUESTION 4

How can working together on instruction make a difference for our students?

Tool 1.7: What does the research say?

By Anne Jolly

PART 1: EFFECTIVE TEACHING MATTERS

"More can be done to improve education by improving the effectiveness of teachers than by any other single factor."
— *Paul Wright, Sandra Horn, & William Sanders, 1997*

Competent, committed, and caring teachers are the single biggest influence on student achievement and the most important factor in preparing students for a 21st-century world. Over the last two decades, evidence continues to mount that teacher quality accounts for the majority of variance in student learning. The 1997 report of the National Commission on Teaching and America's Future, *Doing What Matters Most: Investing in Quality Teaching,* spotlights teacher knowledge and expertise as the most important influence on what students learn. According to the report, teachers who know a lot about teaching and learning and who work in supportive school environments can overcome many of the conditions outside of school that often impair student success.

An analysis of 900 Texas school districts by Harvard professor Ronald Ferguson (1999) confirms teacher expertise as a primary influence on student performance. Researcher Linda Darling-Hammond (1998) points out that the effect of teacher knowledge and skill in this study was so strong that "after controlling for socioeconomic status, the large disparities in achievement between black and white students were almost entirely accounted for by

differences in the qualifications of their teachers."

Groups of students with comparable abilities and initial achievement levels may have vastly different academic outcomes as a result of the teachers to whom they are assigned, according to Eric Hanushek (2002). He discovered that differences in students' annual achievement growth between having a highly effective and an ineffective teacher can be more than one grade level in test performance. Furthermore, students who have ineffective teachers for three consecutive years score as much as 50% lower on achievement tests than those with effective teachers for three consecutive years. William Sanders and June Rivers (1996) found that the residual effects of the type of teaching students received were measurable two years later, regardless of the effectiveness of later teachers.

Teaching quality impacts all students, regardless of their circumstances. A 2001 report by researcher Judith Langer compared student performance in reading, writing, and English in 88 classrooms in California, Florida, New York, and Texas. None of these schools was low-achieving. In fact, all of these schools were characterized by active and engaged students and teachers in well-supported classrooms. Once again, effective teachers had a marked impact on student performance. Over a two-year period, Langer found student achievement to be higher among students with more skilled teachers. In fact, students with the most accomplished teachers achieved at an even higher level than expected.

Such research shines a hopeful light on the

> **What, exactly, defines "teaching expertise"? According to *NSDC's Standards for Staff Development* (2001):**
>
> "Successful teachers have a deep understanding of the subjects they teach, use appropriate instructional methods, and apply various classroom assessment strategies. These teachers participate in sustained, intellectually rigorous professional learning regarding the subjects they teach, the strategies they use to teach those subjects, the findings of cognitive scientists regarding human learning, and the means by which they assess student progress in achieving high academic standards" (p. 32).
>
> No initiative or program a school adopts will substitute for effective teachers who continually build the knowledge, skills, and understanding of today's learners, and who help them master both subject matter and 21st-century skills.

power of effective teachers in terms of student success. According to Ferguson, "Highly qualified teachers have a cumulative effect on students, so that those who score low in the early grades may still achieve at high levels in the upper grades if they have quality teachers." Hanushek (2002) reports that having three years of good teachers in a row can largely overcome the average achievement deficit between low-income students and others. This is energizing news for classroom teachers! Effective teaching can prevail over learning barriers erected by poverty and poor family conditions and can catapult already successful students to greater heights than expected.

Bottom line: Teachers are the most important influence on student learning, and the difference between effective and ineffective teaching is profound. For students to consistently learn and be well-prepared for their world, a school must have teachers who continually work on and improve their own knowledge and expertise in content, current teaching strategies, and assessment.

PART 2: TEACHER OPPORTUNITIES TO LEARN MATTER

"Sustained, intellectually rigorous staff development is essential for everyone who affects students' learning."
— *National Staff Development Council, 2001*

The vast number of our nations' teachers are hard-working, well-educated, and committed to helping students learn and prepare to be successful citizens. So why the increasingly intense national focus on teacher preparation, ongoing learning, and the format and quality of that learning?

Teachers today are working with rapidly shifting student populations whose lives are saturated by the 21st-century media culture. According to Josh McHugh (2005), a survey by the Kaiser Family Foundation found that media use among children and teens skyrocketed with the launch of iPod, instant messaging, mobile video, and YouTube. With the arrival of social networking sites like MySpace, young people are rarely out of contact with media. These

to innovative and effective instructional practices. Additionally, teams where teachers are working together to improve instruction provide an ideal setting for mentoring and inducting new teachers.

Team-based professional learning is indeed powerful, and evidence shows that this type of collaborative learning works well for teachers. According to Hanushek and his co-authors (2005), schools have significant differences in terms of teaching quality. Teachers working together to improve instruction across the board can raise the bar for teachers and level the learning field for students. James Stigler and James Hiebert, authors of *The Teaching Gap* (The Free Press, 1999), analyzed the reasons that working together to prepare and design instruction nets such sizeable benefits for students and teachers in Japan. They discovered that by working in teams, teachers were able to describe and analyze classroom teaching and to teach each other. Working together provided teachers with benchmarks to gauge their own practice and identify ways to improve.

Collaborating with colleagues also creates a new view of teaching as a joint responsibility rather than the responsibility of single individuals. In *Education in a New Era* (ASCD, 2000), Ann Lieberman and Lynn Miller also describe the greater sense of joint responsibility for the success of all students that emerges in collaborative groups. Teachers make the transition from exclusive concerns about "my classroom" and "my students" to a more inclusive attitude about "our school" and "our students."

Team-based professional learning also works for students. To cite several examples, Linda Darling-Hammond in *The Work of Restructuring Schools: Building from the Ground Up* (Teachers College Press, 1995), found that schools where teachers worked together on teaching and learning showed academic

improvement more quickly than schools where this did not happen. A 2005 study (Bolam, McMahon, Stoll, Thomas, & Ingram) of 393 schools and all grade levels found that high-functioning learning teams had a positive impact on both student learning and attendance. Studies by Regina Mistretta (2005) indicate that collaborative learning led to changes in teaching methods and statistically significant gains in student achievement. Work by Susan Trimble (Trimble & Peterson, 2000) also shows changed classroom practices and substantial increases in test scores for students who consistently scored in the lower 25%. In her book, *Professional Learning Communities: Communities of Continuous Inquiry and Improvement* (SEDL, 1997), Shirley Hord presents evidence that a collaborative adult environment leads to more student engagement, fewer tardies, and better attendance.

Bottom line: Collaborative team learning is more effective for teacher and student learning and performance. According to the National Commission on Teaching and America's Future, 21st-century teaching must become a "team sport" (Fulton, Yoon, & Lee, 2005). Simply organizing teachers into teams does not guarantee positive outcomes, however. Many things influence whether teacher teams accomplish something worthwhile for themselves and their students. These include the team's desire for accomplishment, members' understandings of the purpose of the collaboration, the clarity of the goals and focus, and the school conditions in which teachers work. Shirley Hord wisely reminds us (1997) that professional collaboration among teams of teachers can increase teacher effectiveness, but success depends on what the teachers do in their collective efforts.

PART 4: DOING WHAT MATTERS

"Today's young teachers grew up digital. They are ready to meet the challenge of teaching by working with their colleagues and students to transform our factory-era schools into 21st-century learning centers. But they find themselves working alone on self-contained classrooms where they are bound to the teaching practices of the past. Faced with a choice between working in the last century or the 21st century, these new teachers are voting with their feet. The young people we are counting on to teach for the future are leaving our obsolete schools at an alarming rate."

— *Fulton, Yoon, & Lee, 2005*

Change is the most important thing we can accomplish for our next generation of teachers and students — change from an outdated model of education to one that successfully prepares students for a new era. Teachers are leaving the profession today in unprecedented numbers, and recruiting a new generation of teachers by asking them to work in isolation in stand-alone classrooms is not working. The National Commission on Teaching and America's Future report (Fulton, Yoon, & Lee, 2005) reminds us that yesterday's teachers were stand-alone instructors who delivered a fixed body of knowledge and skills to students who used it to engage in predictable careers and pursuits. Today's young citizens are driven by principles of teamwork and smart networking. It's time to incorporate collaboration and teamwork into our schools as a way of organizing teaching and learning.

We know that teachers must increase their effectiveness and expertise in order to prepare students for life in a rapidly-changing 21st-century world. Doing so will be an ongoing process. Teachers must spend more time in professional learning, and much of this learning should occur at the school site. Teachers must work together in a collaborative, intentional manner and support one another in their efforts. Establishing schools where accomplished teaching and learning is occurring requires serious and sustained attention to changing current teaching practices and providing a school organization that allows teachers to collaborate and focus on instruction.

Professional learning teams are a part of the change that must take place if our schools are to become 21st-century learning organizations.

REFERENCES

Bolam, R., McMahon, A., Stoll, L., Thomas, S., & Ingram, M. (2005). *Creating and sustaining effective professional learning communities.* Department for Education and Skills. Research Report RR637. Available at www.dfes.gov.uk/rsgateway/DB/RRP/u013543/index.shtml.

Darling-Hammond, L. (1998). Teacher learning that supports student learning. *Education Leadership, 55*(5), 6-11. Available at www.ascd.org/ed_topics/el199802_darlinghammond.html.

Darling-Hammond, L. (1995). Policy for restructuring, in Ann Lieberman (ed.), *The work of restructuring schools: Building from the ground up.* New York: Teachers College Press.

DuFour, R., Dufour, R., Eaker, R., &

 REFLECT: What are the most powerful points you want to remember from each section of this reading?

Karhanek, G. (2004). *Whatever it takes: How professional learning communities respond when kids don't learn.* Bloomington, IN: Solution Tree.

Ferguson, R. (1999, December 9). *Testimony given in CFE v. State of New York.* Available at www.cfequity.org/Fergus.html

Friedman, T.L. (2006). *The world is flat: A brief history of the 21st century.* New York: Farrar, Straus, & Giroux.

Fulton, K., Yoon, I., & Lee, C. (2005, August). *Induction into learning communities.* Washington, DC: National Commission on Teaching and America's Future.

Hanushek, E. (2002). Teacher quality. In *Teacher Quality,* by L. T. Izumi & W. Evers (Eds.). Stanford, CA: Hoover Institution Press.

Hanushek, E., Kain, J., O'Brien, D., & Rivkin, S. (2005). The market for teacher quality. *NBER Working Paper No. W11154.* Available at http://ssrn.com/abstract=669453.

Hord, S. (1997). *Professional learning communities: Communities of continuous inquiry and improvement.* Austin, TX: Southwest Educational Development Laboratory.

Langer, J. (2001). Beating the odds: Teaching middle and high school students to read and write well. *American Educational Research Journal, 38*(4), 837- 880.

Lewis, L. (2001). *Teacher preparation and professional development: 2000.* Washington, DC: U.S. Department of Education, National Center for Education Statistics. Available at http://nces.ed.gov/surveys/frss/publications/2001088/.

Lieberman, A. & Miller, L. (2000). Teaching and teacher development: A new synthesis for a new century. In *Education in a New Era: 2000 ASCD Yearbook.* Alexandria, VA: ASCD.

McHugh, J. (2005). Synching up with the iKid. *Edutopia.* Available at www.edutopia.org/ikid-digital-learner.

Mistretta, R.M. (2005). Mathematics instructional design: Observations from the field. *The Teacher Educator, 41*(1), 16-33.

National Staff Development Council. (2001). *NSDC's standards for staff development.* Oxford, OH: Author.

Sanders, W. & Rivers, J. (1996). *Cumulative and residual effects of teachers on future student academic achievement.* Available at www.mccsc.edu/~curriculum/cumulative%20and%20residual%20effects%20of%20teachers.pdf.

Scotchmer, M., McGrath, D.J., & Coder, E. (2005). *Characteristics of public school teachers' professional development activities: 1999-2000.* Washington, DC: National Center for Education Statistics. Available at http://nces.ed.gov/pubsearch/pubsinfo.asp?pubid=2005030.

Stigler, J. & Hiebert, J. (1999). *The teaching gap: Best ideas from the world's teachers for improving education in the classroom.* New York: The Free Press.

Trimble, S.B. & Peterson, G.W. (2000). *Multiple team structures and student learning in a high risk middle school.* Paper presented at the annual meeting of the American Educational Research Association, New Orleans, LA. Available at www.eric.ed.gov/ERICDocs/data/ericdocs2sql/content_storage_01/0000019b/80/16/4a/41.pdf.

U.S. Department of Education. (2000). *A talented, dedicated, and well-prepared teacher in every classroom.* Washington, DC: Author. Available at www.eric.ed.gov/ERICDocs/data/ericdocs2sql/content_storage_01/0000019b/80/16/5b/c0.pdf.

Tool 2.1: Professional learning team FAQs

Directions: Read about professional learning teams, then share your thoughts about these teams with a colleague.

WHAT ARE PROFESSIONAL LEARNING TEAMS?

Professional learning teams are small groups of teachers working together to learn more about teaching and build new instructional skills to accomplish needed results. These teachers meet on a long-term, regular basis (preferably at least one hour per week). Professional learning team meetings focus exclusively on teacher professional learning and growth.

WHO IS PART OF A TEAM?

Teams may form around grade levels, disciplines, topics, or other commonalities. They may be interdisciplinary or organize around other criteria. Teams should be small enough that all team members can actively participate, share leadership, and build supportive relationships. Teams with three to five members usually work well together.

WHEN AND WHERE DO TEAMS MEET?

Optimally, teams meet at the school during the school day. Meeting space should be as comfortable and free from interruption as possible.

> "Isolation of teachers is so ingrained in the traditional culture of schools that invitations to collaborate are insufficient. To build professional learning communities, meaningful collaboration must be systematically embedded into the daily life of the school."
>
> **Source:** *Professional Learning Communities at Work,* by Richard DuFour and Robert Eaker. Bloomington, IN: Solution Tree, 1998, p. 118.

WHAT DO TEAM MEMBERS DO?

Team members:

1. **Examine student achievement and classroom data** to make decisions about what teachers need to learn and what new skills they need to help students learn.
2. **Develop a shared instructional goal** based on identified student needs.
3. **Establish shared norms** and values that spell out the expectations and interpersonal skills team members will use during team meetings.
4. **Study and learn** about research-based instructional practices that can help them meet student learning needs.
5. **Build supportive relationships** with colleagues and a culture of openness and shared responsibility for effective teaching and learning.
6. **Rotate leadership responsibilities** to build joint ownership in the team's work and expand leadership skills.

7. **Work together** to examine current instruction, develop new or improved teaching materials and approaches, and implement new classroom strategies. Team members monitor progress, observe one another, examine student responses and work, and engage in other activities that move them toward more effective and accomplished teaching.

8. **Analyze** the results of their efforts and adjust their teaching practices based on collective reflection and wisdom.

9. **Communicate** information about learning team activities with the faculty, administration, parents, and others as appropriate. Teams document big ideas and decisions from their meetings as one way of sharing their work with others and creating avenues for conversation among school staff about instruction.

REFLECT: In what ways do professional learning team meetings differ from other types of meetings at your school?

_____

_____

_____

_____

REFLECT: What value do you think these meeting might have for teachers? For students?

_____

_____

_____

_____

Source: "Use time for faculty study," by Carlene U. Murphy. (1999). *Journal of Staff Development, 20*(2).

Tool 2.2: Terms that describe professional learning teams

Collaborative	These meetings engage teachers in working together to increase their teaching expertise.
Communication	Team members keep written records (logs) of team discussions and decisions and use these as a tool for sharing information.
Continual learning	Cutting-edge teaching requires updating knowledge and skills on an ongoing basis.
Data-driven	Instructional practices are revised and adapted based on an analysis of student data and information.
Experimental	Team members experiment with new instructional practices, analyze them, and adjust them.
Evidence-based	Teams build their instruction on studies of practices that have been tested and found to be effective.
Goal	Team goals focus teacher learning and growth.
Instructional focus	Meetings focus exclusively and only on improving classroom instruction.
Job-embedded	Meetings occur at the school site and during the school day.
Norms	Teams establish ground rules and procedures for working together.
Public practice	Team members open their classrooms and make their teaching visible to colleagues.
Purposeful	Professional learning team meetings focus on improving existing classroom practices and generating new teaching practices to increase student learning.
Reflective	Teams engage in rigorous reflection and questioning about teaching and learning.
Shared leadership	Team responsibilities rotate weekly or monthly.
Systematic	Meetings occur on a regular basis, preferably at least once a week.

Tool 2.3: The professional learning team decision-making cycle

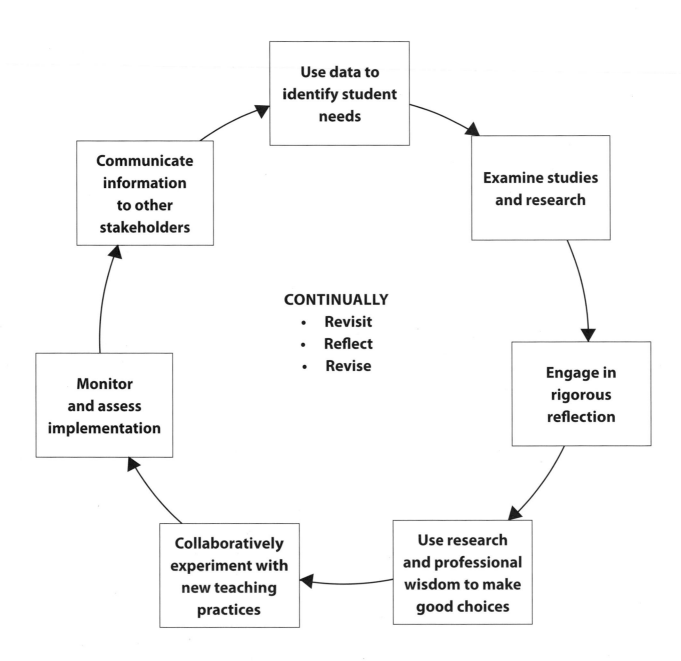

Use data to identify student needs

Examine studies and research

Engage in rigorous reflection

Use research and professional wisdom to make good choices

Collaboratively experiment with new teaching practices

Monitor and assess implementation

Communicate information to other stakeholders

CONTINUALLY
- Revisit
- Reflect
- Revise

Adapted from the Evidence Based Decisionmaking Cycle, SERVE Center at the University of North Carolina at Greensboro.

Tool 2.4a: Table tent question 1

Directions: Create table tents with the question on the next page and use it as a reminder in team meetings.

Is the focus on teacher learning and growth?

¿Is the focus on teacher learning and growth?

Tool 2.4b: Appropriate use of learning teams

Directions: Put a check mark under the appropriate column for whether you think the statement accurately describes professional learning teams' work. Thumbs-up indicates you agree; thumbs-down means you disagree. When you are finished, discuss your responses with the group.

Professional learning teams:

	👍	👎
1. Keep the same team members all year.		
2. Focus on school improvement issues.		
3. Coordinate and improve classroom teaching strategies.		
4. Keep the same focus for the entire school year.		
5. Work on curriculum alignment and mapping.		
6. Examine student work and analyze student thinking.		
7. Look at and apply research-based information on teaching.		
8. Focus on classroom management and discipline.		
9. Meet at the school and during the school day.		
10. Examine the impact of new teaching strategies on students.		
11. Include the principal as a member of the team.		
12. Rotate responsibilities among team members.		
13. Focus on teacher professional learning and growth.		
14. Discuss department or grade-level issues.		
15. Observe colleagues using relevant teaching strategies.		
16. Attend all learning team meetings.		
17. Document team activities and discussions in a meeting log.		
18. Work on procedures for improving standardized test scores.		
19. Discuss administrative and front-burner issues.		
20. Share team logs and accomplishments schoolwide.		
21. Keep the team size small (three to five members).		
22. Study a book about instruction (book study).		
23. Meet on an as-needed basis.		
24. Keep a focus on classroom instruction.		
25. Periodically evaluate team functioning.		

Tool 2.5: Meeting overview checklist

Directions: There is no single way to conduct learning team meetings. This list suggests ideas for some activities. Refer to this list periodically for ideas that might have value for your team. Include as many activities as possible throughout the year.

ALL MEETINGS

- Communicate! Keep records (logs) of all team meetings. Include big ideas from the meeting discussions, decisions made, and plans for the next meeting. After each meeting, e-mail the log or post it on a school wiki. Read logs from other teams and offer insights.
- Plan the next meeting.

INITIAL MEETING(S)

- Take care of team logistics.
- Set team norms.
- Determine a team goal.
  1. Look at a variety of student data and information.
  2. Decide on an area in which teachers need to increase their expertise, based on where students need the most help.
  3. Plan an initial course of action.
  4. Determine what information and resources are needed.

CONTINUING MEETINGS

- Examine research and information (books, articles, etc.).
- Share, develop, and/or modify instructional practices to address student needs.
- Coordinate and systematically apply new instructional practices in classrooms.
- Monitor student responses.
- Reflect on and discuss classroom applications and make needed adjustments.

POSSIBLE MEETING ACTIVITIES

- Develop joint or coordinated lessons.
- Examine student written work.
- Examine videotapes or DVDs of student responses to particular activities.
- Examine teacher assignments.
- Observe other team members or teachers using specific activities with students.
- Observe a videotape or DVD of a colleague implementing a particular strategy.
- Discuss the effectiveness of teaching strategies and approaches.
- Monitor the team's progress toward instructional goals.
- Monitor the team's functioning as a collaborative group.
- Keep the team's work public. Post logs on web sites, e-mail logs and activities schoolwide, engage other teachers, run ideas by the faculty, and honor their input.
- Develop a tool kit of information and practices that can serve as a resource for other teachers.
- Modify and improve the professional learning team process throughout the year.

REFLECT: Keep a list of additional activities in which your learning team engages over the course of the year, and make these ideas available to other teams.

Tool 2.6a: What did you see and hear?

Directions: As you watch the skit, observe how teachers interact. Jot down your thoughts in the space below. Share your ideas with colleagues.

A.   How teachers interact with one another.

_____

_____

_____

_____

B.   What types of conversations team members have.

_____

_____

_____

_____

C.   The kinds of activities team members engage in.

_____

_____

_____

_____

D.   Things that seem to make the meeting successful.

_____

_____

_____

_____

 REFLECT: After watching this skit, discuss your observations with colleagues. Together make a list of things you noticed about this professional learning team meeting. Prepare to share your ideas.

Tool 2.6b: Professional learning team meeting skit

Directions: Read the part for which you have volunteered or been selected. Be dramatic, and have fun with it.

Team members sit in the designated area, with coffee cups, notebooks, and pens in hand.

Narrator: Teachers do not normally work together on a regular basis to examine their teaching practice closely, so knowing exactly what to do during learning team time may be puzzling, at least at first. To give you an idea of what might go on, consider this *highly contrived* scenario.

Meet today's team members: Sue, Maria, Chris, and Juan. Each one teaches a different subject — science, math, social studies, and language arts. They meet during the school day for one hour each week. These learning team members have already met several times. They've decided on a team goal — to learn more effective methods of helping students read and understand their textbooks. They also have set some ground rules for how their meetings will run.

As team members take their seats, Maria volunteers to record today's big ideas from the team's discussions, along with any decision the team makes, in a team log. Today's team leader, Sue, begins the meeting.

Sue: Several weeks ago, we kicked off our learning team by analyzing several types of data for our students. The data verify what we already know — our students need help in reading comprehension. Many of them don't read their assignments. Even when they do, some of them struggle and don't understand what they read. So we decided to work together this year to learn how to help our kids understand what they read in all of their subjects. We are going to start by using a book that has some research-based ideas that may work for us. This week, we all read the chapter on how to diagnose our students' reading needs. What is it, exactly, that they can't do? Chris, you volunteered to lead today's discussion.

Chris: Well, as I started looking at all the things that good readers can do, I was amazed. I'm a good reader, but I didn't realize I was doing all of these things. Take a look at page 17.

Narrator: For the next 15 minutes, Chris and the other team members share information and ideas on assessing students' needs in reading. Then Maria, the math teacher, comments:

Maria: This is really helpful. A lot of my students can't handle reading math problems. This gives me a way to diagnose where their comprehension is breaking down. And it gives me ideas for specific strategies to help them conquer those problems.

Chris: I feel the same way. But I have a question. While we're in the process of diagnosing our students' individual reading problems, should we go ahead and start using some of these reading strategies in our classrooms?

Juan: I'd say yes, we should definitely do that. I've scanned the book, and there are several strategies there that I think would help all of my students.

Sue: So, exactly which of these strategies are we going to work with first?

Narrator: Team members discuss various reading strategies they could use with their students. They agree to begin by all working with prereading strategies.

Juan: OK, so what now? Do you want me to look for more information on prereading strategies before our next meeting and come up with additional suggestions for how to use these in our classrooms?

Chris: Sounds good to me. In the meantime, I'll use the information in this chapter to draft a checklist we might use to diagnose our students' reading difficulties. That will help us target our reading strategies better.

Sue: Hey, I just had another idea. One of our teachers, Ms. Duke, conducts workshops on reading comprehension strategies. Why don't I invite her to one of our team meetings to give us all some tips?

Narrator: Team members like Sue's idea and decide to ask Ms. Duke to be a resource for them throughout the year.

Sue: OK, let's review where we are. We've decided to start by learning how to diagnose our students' reading problems. While we are doing that, we will also be learning some ways of helping them prepare to read a selection from their textbooks.

Juan: You nailed it, but are we moving fast enough with this? I mean, what are we going to do in our classrooms this week? What if the principal comes in and says, "Hey, Juan! What are you doing to help your kids with reading?"

Maria: *(Waving the log in the air.)* That's one reason we have this log. It gives us a record of when we're meeting and what we're learning. Hey! Did you guys read the copy of last week's log that we e-mailed to the principal? He really read it! Did you see the message he e-mailed back to us?

Sue: Yeah, these logs really come in handy. The principal doesn't have to sit in here and meet with us to know what's going on.

[All nod vigorously.]

Juan: And it gives us a way to communicate regularly with him. He really does seem to like what we're doing. Hey, speaking of communicating, did you see that several teachers from other learning teams replied to the log we e-mailed? The 6th-grade team even sent us an article they came across to use as a resource.

Narrator: Team members agree that sharing logs is a good way to build a sense of community within the faculty and to share ideas and expertise.

Maria: Here's something else we need to think about. How are we going to know that the strategies we use really help our students understand what they read? What kind of evidence are we going to collect during the year?

Narrator: The team discusses different kinds of evidence they can gather, and Maria volunteers to call the reading specialist for additional ideas to bring back to the team at the next meeting.

Juan: You know, I can put together a web page where we can post information about reading strategies and assignments, along with examples of what our kids are doing.

Chris: What a great idea! Want to post our team logs there also? Then our students and parents can see what we're doing. The kids can see that we believe learning is important, because we're learning, too.

Narrator: The team agrees that a web page would be a valuable resource, and that continual learning is an important concept they can model for their students.

Sue: OK, now let's recap what we've done. We're going to focus on two areas: diagnosing specific reading difficulties our students have and working together on some prereading strategies. Juan is going to get more information on prereading strategies before our next meeting. Chris will draft a checklist to help us get started with assessing our students' difficulties. I will ask Ms. Duke to meet with our team, and I'll also see if I can observe her using some prereading strategies. Maria will talk to the reading specialist to get ideas on how to tell if we're making a difference for students. Juan will start developing a web page. Now, who wants to be the team leader next week?

Maria: What does the leader do?

Sue: Well, as this week's team leader, I checked with all of you to be sure you remembered this meeting. I reminded Chris that he was going to lead today's book discussion. I also asked the office folks not to interrupt us during the meeting. Basically, I just tried to keep the meeting on everybody's front burner. Once we got here, I tried to keep us on track.

Maria: I guess I can do that next week.

Sue: Great! Thanks, Maria. Now, does anyone have any concerns or recommendations about today's meeting?

Juan: I'm just glad I have you guys to help me as I muddle through this. I'm a science teacher. I'm not that good at teaching reading right now.

Maria: Hey, we're all going to muddle through this together. None of us alone is as good as all of us together! Uh-oh — it's time for the bell.

Narrator: Grabbing their now-empty coffee cups, team members head for their classrooms.

Tool 3.1: The ideal start-up

Directions: Answer the questions below to generate ideas about what would ideally be in place for a successful rollout of professional learning teams. While these ideas may not materialize, the gap between the actual and the ideal can provide useful information for planning purposes and can help you identify issues to address early on.

1. Ideally, what knowledge, skills, and information about professional learning teams would teachers have?

_____

_____

_____

_____

_____

2. Ideally, what attitudes would teachers have about participating in professional learning teams?

_____

_____

_____

_____

_____

3. Ideally, what school policies and procedures would be in place to support professional learning teams?

_____

_____

_____

_____

_____

4. Ideally, what incentives would be in place to support professional learning teams?

_____

_____

_____

_____

_____

Tool 3.2: Support structures for professional learning teams

Directions: How ready is your school to begin the professional learning team initiative? Do a quick front-end analysis to see how many of these factors that influence team performance are in place. Place a check mark in the box next to items you agree currently describe your school. Discuss which boxes you checked in small groups. Which items can be addressed prior to beginning professional learning teams? Which will need attention during the course of the initiative?

TEACHER KNOWLEDGE, SKILLS, AND INFORMATION

The faculty knows:

❏ How to collaborate with other adults.
❏ Why teachers are using professional learning teams.
❏ How learning teams are structured.
❏ What to do in a learning team meeting.
❏ How to manage resistance and conflict.
❏ How teachers can get needed information, resources, and assistance.

TEACHER MOTIVATION AND COMMITMENT

The faculty:

❏ Sees professional learning teams as relevant.
❏ Values the opportunity to work collaboratively.
❏ Feels confident teachers can succeed in this initiative.
❏ Exhibits enthusiasm.
❏ Believes this effort will help students.

SCHOOL ENVIRONMENT, TOOLS, AND PROCESSES

❏ Policies and procedures are in place that will support learning teams.
❏ The school culture and organization are structured in a way that makes learning teams a natural outcome.
❏ Resources are available.
❏ Existing teacher workloads and expectations allow for learning team work.
❏ Teachers' noninstructional responsibilities are minimal.

INCENTIVES

The school will encourage learning team participation through:

❏ Memberships in professional organizations and education journal subscriptions.
❏ Conferences and workshop attendance as teams or groups.
❏ Opportunities for learning team presentations.
❏ Celebrations, appreciation, and high team visibility.
❏ Exchanges (e.g. professional learning credit, business cards, time trades).
❏ Frequent feedback.
❏ Involvement in decision making about professional learning teams.
❏ Adjusted teacher workloads.
❏ Spotlighting team successes.
❏ Spotlighting student successes.

Tool 3.3: Learning team options

Directions: Discuss each option and record your thinking. Which option would ideally produce the best results for your students? Which are realistic for your staff?

Option	Description	Student learning needs that could be addressed with this option	Advantages/disadvantages of this option
Faculty-wide teams	The entire faculty participates in learning teams focused on the same initiative.		
Special topic teams	Teachers group themselves in teams around topics of interest that relate to instruction.		
Interdisciplinary teams	Teams of teachers who share common planning times and the same students work together.		
Grade-level teams	Teachers work together on effective instructional practices for students at a particular grade level.		
Vertical teams	Teachers work together across grade levels to address specific student needs across grades.		
Subject-area teams	Teachers address instructional and learning needs within their subject areas.		
Between-school teams	Teachers from different schools work together on a common initiative.		

Tool 3.4: Team logistics

Directions: Use this activity to help with initial team logistics. Work with other team members to brainstorm ideas for each question. The bullet points in the column at left suggest issues you may need to consider in making these decisions. After discussing each question in the column on the right, write the team's decisions in the space provided beneath each question.

Guidelines and suggestions	Decisions
• Keep team small (three to five people). • Consider personalities, diversity of ideas, and teaching styles, forming a critical mass of positive people. • "Teachers only" is recommended; however, to get off to a good start, teams may begin by using a different composition.	**Who is on our professional learning team?**
• Meeting during the school day lends value and credibility to the process.	**When will our team meet?**
• At the school, in comfortable surroundings. • In an area safe from interruptions. • In an area where teachers can sit facing each other.	**Where will our team meet?**
• Access to computer during meetings. • Articles, books, and other sources of information about the topic of study. • Basic supplies (pens, sticky notes). • A team notebook (three-ring binder) and a set of tabs.	**What resources will our team need to begin?**
• A process and schedule for rotating team roles and responsibilities.	**Who will be team leader and recorder?**
• A variety of methods for communicating with other teams and the principal.	**What methods of communicating our work will we use?**

Tool 3.5: Time to meet

Directions: Place a check mark by ideas that appeal to you and an asterisk (*) by those you think are most workable for your school. Talk over your choices with others from your school or with nearby participants.

BANK TIME

❏ Lengthen the regular school day. Save the extra minutes to create larger blocks of time when teachers can plan or learn together.

❏ Adjust arrival and dismissal times so that school begins 30 minutes early on Monday through Thursday and dismisses two hours early on Friday for teachers to have time to meet collaboratively each Friday.

❏ Create regularly scheduled early dismissal/late start days.

❏ Shave minutes off the lunch period and save that time for teacher learning time.

❏ Total the number of hours teachers meet after school in learning teams, and do not require teachers to report to school for that amount of time on regularly scheduled teacher workdays.

BUY TIME

❏ Use paraprofessionals to release teachers during the school day for meetings.

❏ Hire a team of rotating substitute teachers to release teachers and enable them to plan or learn together.

❏ Hire one or two permanent subs to fill in regularly for teachers to free them for professional learning team meetings.

❏ Schedule a team of substitute teachers for a day a week to release teachers on a rotating basis for learning team meetings.

❏ Hire more teachers, clerks, and support staff to expand or add learning time for teachers.

USE COMMON TIME

❏ Use common planning time to enable teachers working with the same students, the same grade level, or the same subjects to meet in professional learning teams.

❏ Organize special subjects into blocks of time to create common time for teachers to meet.

❏ Link planning periods to other noninstructional times, such as lunch periods, giving teachers the option of using time for shared learning.

❏ Create double planning periods.

USE RESOURCE PERSONNEL FOR STUDENT LEARNING ACTIVITIES

❏ Enlist administrators to teach classes.

❏ Allow teaching assistants and/or college interns to monitor classes.

❏ Pair teachers so one teaches while the other meets with his/her professional learning team.

❏ Plan off-site field experiences for students and use the block of time created for teacher professional learning team meetings.

❏ Ask parent volunteers to take classes for an hour for a learning team to meet.

❏ Arrange educational activities for students led by professionals from local colleges, businesses, governmental agencies, or community agencies, and use this time for professional learning team meetings.

FREE TEACHERS FROM NONINSTRUCTIONAL REQUIREMENTS

❏ Use non-homeroom teachers to occasionally perform homeroom duties so teachers can meet for an extended time before school and through homeroom.

❏ Reassign school personnel to allow teachers to meet during pep rallies and assemblies.

❏ Provide more time for teachers to engage in collaborative work by removing noninstructional administrative, clerical, and school management tasks from teachers' duties and encouraging teams to use that extra time to meet and focus intently on instruction.

ADD PROFESSIONAL DAYS TO THE SCHOOL YEAR

❏ Create multiday summer learning institutes for teachers to give them needed depth in the areas of focus for the professional learning teams.

❏ Create a midyear break for students, and use those days for teacher learning.

USE EXISTING TIME MORE EFFECTIVELY

❏ Set aside faculty meeting times for professional learning, and put all general faculty announcements in newsletters and/or e-mails to teachers.

❏ Spread time from existing planning days across the calendar to provide more frequent, shorter school-based opportunities to learn.

Reflect: Your thoughts, please! Which options do you prefer? What other ideas do you have?

_____

_____

_____

_____

_____

Reflect: Which options do you think are most able to be accomplished from the school's standpoint?

_____

_____

_____

_____

Source: "Think outside the clock: Create time for professional learning," by Joan Richardson. (2002, August/September). *Tools for Schools,* 1-2.

Tool 3.6: Resources on time

Directions: Here are resources for additional information on finding time for professional learning. You can also go to an Internet search engine and type in "finding time for professional development."

NATIONAL STAFF DEVELOPMENT COUNCIL

See www.nsdc.org/library/resources/time.cfm. This site has many articles on finding time, including:

- **"Finding time for faculties to study together," by Carlene Murphy. (1997, Summer).** *Journal of Staff Development, 18*(3). Murphy states that if a faculty agrees that schools are learning organizations for the adults in the building as well as for children, time will be found. She cites numerous examples of real schools that are finding time for professional learning.

- **"Think outside the clock: Create time for professional learning," by Joan Richardson. (2002, August/September).** *Tools for Schools,* 1-2. Richardson offers examples of real schools that have made time for teachers to learn during the school day. She cites experiences of staff developers and consultants who offer insights into the problems and possibilities of finding time.

- **"Target time toward teachers," by Linda Darling-Hammond. (1999, Spring).** *Journal of Staff Development, 20*(2). Darling-Hammond writes about numerous schools that have restructured for ongoing professional development. She discusses strategies that (1) allow for shared planning, (2) support stronger relationships and deeper knowledge of learners, and (3) create longer blocks of instructional time while reducing teaching loads and increasing planning time.

- *Finding Time for Professional Learning,* **by Valerie von Frank, Ed. Oxford, OH: NSDC, 2008.** This compilation of articles and tools about time features ideas and articles published in NSDC's newsletters and *JSD* during the last decade. It includes suggestions about how to use the articles to guide the discussion about time in your school and district.

- **"Time: It's made, not found," by Stephen Barkley. (1999, Fall).** *Journal of Staff Development, 20*(4). Barkley argues that school reform is slowed due to lack of time for professional learning. He cites examples of making time, including periodically regrouping students into larger classes, thus freeing up as many as half the faculty to meet together.

ERIC CLEARINGHOUSE

Go to www/eric.ed.gov and type "time for teacher professional development" in the "search terms" box. Select "title" under the "search in" area. Click "search" and bring up a variety of articles on finding time.

LEARNING POINT ASSOCIATES

Go to www.learningpt.org and type "finding time for professional development" in the search engine at that site. The site offers a variety of resources and information for creating time for professional learning during the school day.

NATIONAL COMMISSION ON TIME AND LEARNING

- *Prisoners of Time,* **by the National Education Commission on Time and Learning. Washington, DC: Author, 1994.** This is an excellent resource for thoroughly examining the challenge of time for teaching and learning. The Commission makes realistic, powerful recommendations concerning the use of time as a factor to support learning, not a boundary that marks its limits. The entire document is available online at www.ed.gov/pubs/PrisonersOfTime/.

Tool 3.7: Sample timeline for implementing professional learning teams

Directions: This timeline is based on a guide for implementing professional learning teams created by Linda Winburn for the Richland 2 School District in Colombia, S.C. Review this school implementation timeline with your principal and faculty, and use the example to create your own implementation guide. Revisit your plan periodically and adjust it as needed as implementation proceeds.

JUNE ACTIVITIES

1. Meet with teachers and administrators to discuss and plan for improving student achievement and teaching quality through professional learning teams.
2. Identify teacher leaders to assist with supporting professional learning teams at the school.
3. Collect data so teams can identify needs and establish goals.

AUGUST ACTIVITIES

1. Provide professional learning team information and facilitation training to identified teacher leaders.
2. Give all participating faculty the pre/post survey.
3. Introduce the concept of professional learning teams to faculty.
4. Engage school staff in planning and organizing learning teams in a manner best suited for your school. Set weekly team meeting times and locations; identify team members, and note needed resources.
5. Train school faculty in the professional learning team process.
6. Provide teachers with information, assistance, and tools for implementing and sustaining productive learning teams.
7. Identify administrators and faculty who will receive team meeting logs (one per team). Include team members and the principal.
8. Begin professional learning team meetings by the end of August or first of September. Teams will begin by:
   a. Defining team expectations/setting norms (Step 4).
   b. Looking at student data (Step 5).
   c. Deciding on a team goal and designing a plan (Steps 5 and 6).
   These steps will take several meetings. Keep encouraging the teams.
9. Forward team logs to the principal, team members, and other identified recipients. The principal will provide brief feedback on each team log. Others also may provide some feedback.

SEPTEMBER THROUGH MAY

1. Begin full implementation of professional learning teams. Teams study, develop plans for increasing teacher expertise and quality instruction, experiment with new teaching practices in the classroom, reflect on results, and make needed adjustments.
2. Continue forwarding team meeting logs to the school principal, team members, and other designees. When the teachers are comfortable with the process, ask teams to forward their logs to the entire school faculty.

Tool 4.1: Traits of successful team members

Directions: Use the following scale to rate each statement in terms of how well you think it describes — or will describe — you as a current or future team member. (You may write the numbers or simply make a mental note of your score.) Add comments to explain or clarify your thinking.

4 – All of the time   3 – Most of the time   2 – Some of the time   1 – None of the time

1. I am committed to the professional learning team and its goals. ____
   _____
   _____

2. I show respect and understanding toward other team members. ____
   _____
   _____

3. I am willing to help, support, and trust other team members. ____
   _____
   _____

4. I participate in a way that creates a comfortable atmosphere for sharing both successes and failures. ____
   _____
   _____

5. I have a high tolerance for discussion, debate, and disagreement. ____
   _____
   _____

6. I am willing to question, get outside my current mindset, and be open to new ideas and solutions. ____
   _____
   _____

7. I value my team members and their input. ____
   _____
   _____

8. I share in team leadership and other team responsibilities. ____
   _____
   _____

Norms put the 'Golden Rule' into practice for groups

By Joan Richardson

Lillian always arrives late and thinks nothing of chatting with her seatmate while someone else is trying to make a point. Arthur routinely reads a newspaper during each meeting. Barbara can't wait until each meeting ends so she can head to the parking lot to tell someone what she could have said during the meeting.

Later, most of them grumble that "these meetings are just a waste of my time. We never get anything accomplished."

Having a set of norms — or ground rules — that a group follows encourages behaviors that will help a group do its work and discourages behaviors that interfere with a group's effectiveness.

Think of norms as "a behavior contract," said Kathryn Blumsack, an educational consultant from Maryland who specializes in team development.

Norms are the unwritten rules for how we act and what we do. They are the rules that govern how we interact with each other, how we conduct business, how we make decisions, how we communicate, even how we dress when we get together.

"Norms are part of the culture. They exist whether or not you acknowledge them. They exist whether or not you formalize them," Blumsack said.

Pat Roy, director of the Delaware Professional Development Center, said identifying a set of norms is an effective way to democratize a group. Writing norms helps create groups that are able to have honest discussions that enable everyone to participate and be heard, she said.

WHO NEEDS NORMS?

Any group that meets regularly or that is trying to "do business" needs to identify its existing norms or develop new norms. In school districts, that would include department groups, grade-level teams, interdisciplinary teams, content-area teams, school improvement teams, action teams, curriculum committees, leadership teams, advisory committees, and special project groups.

Although a group can pause and set norms at any time, Blumsack and Roy agree that it's ideal

Source: "Norms put the 'Golden Rule' into practice for groups," by Joan Richardson. (1999, August/September). *Tools for Schools,* 1-2.

to set norms at the beginning of a group's work together.

"If you don't set norms at the beginning, when the behaviors become ineffective, you have a harder time pulling behavior back to where it should be," Roy said.

Because every group has unspoken norms for behavior, groups need to work at being explicit about what they expect from each other. "Get those assumptions out on the table," Blumsack said.

CREATING NORMS

Some groups would prefer to have a set of norms handed to them. But Roy and Blumsack both said groups will feel more ownership of the norms if they identify and write their own.

"If they don't do this, 10 minutes after you've handed them a list, they'll begin violating the norms because they aren't their norms," Roy said.

There are two distinct ways to write norms. The first is by observing and writing down the norms that already are in use.

That's how the NSDC Board of Trustees established the set of norms it has used for about eight years. The NSDC board meets for two days twice a year, each time with a lengthy agenda of material that must be addressed.

The norms grew out of a board discussion about how it operated and how it wanted to operate. Pat Roy, who was then a board member, was tapped to observe the board's implicit norms during one meeting and draft a set of norms. "Essentially, I wrote down what I saw in operation," Roy said.

Roy's first draft was edited and refined by staff and other board members. That set of initial norms has been largely unchanged over the years.

The second way is to have group members suggest ideal behaviors for groups, eventually refining those suggested behaviors into a set of norms.

Blumsack cautions that norms must fit the group. Not every group would feel comfortable with the same set of rules, which is why each group must create its own rules, she said.

For example, she recently worked with a group that was "very chatty, very extroverted." Initially, the group wanted a norm that banned side conversations. Two days into their work, the group was frustrated because Blumsack, as the facilitator, kept trying to enforce the norm against side conversations. Finally, the group agreed to modify the norm to fit its unique personality. Their new norm was: "If you need to make a comment, do so but return quickly to the main conversation."

PUBLICIZING THE NORMS

Simply writing norms does not guarantee that the group will remember and respect them. Groups need to continually remind themselves about the norms they've identified.

At a minimum, the norms should be posted in the group's meeting room, Roy said. "Post them and celebrate them," she said.

Blumsack recommends creating tented name cards for each group member. On the side facing out, write the group member's name; on the side facing the member, print the group's norms.

Source: "Norms put the 'Golden Rule' into practice for groups," by Joan Richardson. (1999, August/September). *Tools for Schools*, 1-2.

The NSDC board receives a list of its norms along with materials for each of its twice-a-year board meetings. Then, at the beginning of each meeting, the president reintroduces the norms to reacquaint board members with them. Since new board members join each year, this also helps to acculturate newcomers with the board's expectations.

Sometimes the board uses activities to aid in that. During one meeting, for example, each board member was asked to illustrate one norm and the others tried to identify the norms based on those illustrations. Those illustrations were then taped to the meeting room's walls as visual reminders to be vigilant about the norms. Another time, board members were asked to write down as many board norms as they could recall from memory.

ENFORCING THE NORMS

Perhaps the toughest part of living with norms is having the norms enforced.

"The reality is that every group will violate every norm at one time or another. So you have to talk about violations and how you'll deal with them," Roy said.

Blumsack agrees. "If you don't call attention to the fact that a norm has been violated, in effect you're creating a second set of norms. For example, a common norm is expecting everyone to be on time. If you don't point out when someone violates that norm, then, in effect, you're saying that it's really not important to be on time," Blumsack said.

After a group identifies its norms, they suggest asking how they would like to be notified that they have violated a norm.

Roy recommends finding light, humorous ways to point out violations. One group she worked with kept a basket of foam rubber balls in the middle of the table. Violation of a norm meant being pelted with foam rubber balls. Other groups have used small colored cards, flags, or hankies that could be waved when a violation was noted.

Having all group members take responsibility for enforcing the norm is key, Blumsack said. Enforcing the norms should not be just the job of the group's leader.

EVALUATING THE NORMS

Finally, each group needs to periodically evaluate its adherence to the norms. A group that meets once or twice a year might evaluate each time they meet; a group that meets weekly might evaluate once a month or so.

Blumsack recommends giving each group member an opportunity to speak about what he or she has observed or take each statement and ask group members, "How well did we do on this norm?"

Each member should be encouraged to identify the group's areas of strength as well as its areas of weakness, but not to single out violators.

"The more up front you are about how the group is doing, the easier it will be to communicate about the other issues you're dealing with," Blumsack said.■

Source: "Norms put the 'Golden Rule' into practice for groups," by Joan Richardson. (1999, August/ September). *Tools for Schools,* 1-2.

Tool 4.3: A norm sampler

Directions: Read each norm created by an imaginary learning team at Norton High School. Place a check mark next to norms you believe will help these teachers operate efficiently and productively as a team. Discuss with a partner what other norms you might suggest.

What rules will govern attendance?

- ❏ Each team member will commit to participate actively for the school year.
- ❏ All members will arrive on time and stay for the entire meeting.
- ❏ We will start on time and end on time.

What rules will govern how we talk together?

- ❏ All members will join in the team's discussions.
- ❏ No one will dominate the discussions.
- ❏ Each member will listen attentively as others speak.
- ❏ Everyone's point of view will be considered.
- ❏ Our conversations will reflect our respect for and acceptance of one another.
- ❏ We will disagree with ideas, not individuals.
- ❏ No zingers or put-downs.
- ❏ We will keep confidential any information shared in confidence.

What other expectations do we have for team members?

- ❏ We will rotate the team leader role.
- ❏ All members will be prepared for the meeting when they arrive.
- ❏ All members will be "totally present" during the meeting.
- ❏ All members will refrain from grading papers and working on other things during the meeting.
- ❏ All members will refrain from scheduling other activities during the meeting time.
- ❏ All members will turn off cell phones.
- ❏ All members will stay on task during the meeting.
- ❏ All members will work to keep team meetings positive and productive.
- ❏ The atmosphere will remain cordial and friendly throughout the meeting.
- ❏ We will have fun and enjoy working together.

What decision-making procedures will we use?

- ❏ We will reach decisions by consensus.

How will we assess our team functioning?

- ❏ We will briefly revisit our norms after each meeting or two and decide which ones we need to follow better and which we need to change.

Tool 4.4: Considerations for team norms

Directions: As you begin working together, think about ground rules that might guide the way your team does business. Several categories are suggested here. Read each question and make suggestions in the column on the right, then discuss your ideas with your team members.

CONSIDERATIONS	IDEAS FOR NORMS
What procedures will govern meeting attendance? *Consider:* • Will team members be dependable and committed for the entire year? • Will team members arrive on time and stay for the entire meeting? • Will they stay on task, avoid side conversations and interruptions, and focus on the task at hand?	
What procedures will govern teacher dialogue? *Consider:* • How will team members react to others' work and ideas? • Are out-of-the-box and off-the-wall ideas welcome? • Are differing opinions welcome? • Will what members say be held in confidence? • How will the team encourage listening and discourage interrupting?	
What rules will govern decision making? *Consider:* • Will the team reach decisions by consensus? • How will members deal with conflicts and differences of opinion?	

CONSIDERATIONS	IDEAS FOR NORMS
What attitudes and behaviors do you expect from team members? *Consider:* • Are all team members expected to be prepared and to participate? • Should they be "fully present," both mentally and physically? • Will they put away other work (grading papers, filling out reports, etc.)? • Should team members try to convey positive attitudes? • Will team members try to maintain a sense of humor?	
How often will your team evaluate its functioning, and what indicators will you evaluate? *Consider:* • Are team members abiding by the team's agreed-upon norms? • What ground rules did you use well? • What norms do you need to re-emphasize, add, or adjust?	

Tool 4.5: Develop team norms

Directions: Use this process to jump-start your thinking about useful team norms that will enhance interpersonal skills, trust, and respect among team members. When team members have completed the handout, share your responses as a group. On chart paper, list the behaviors and norms on which you all agree. Then consider the remaining norms, and reach consensus on others that may be important to include at this time.

List six behaviors you value in others during team meetings.

1. _____

2. _____

3. _____

4. _____

5. _____

6. _____

What norms could your team put in place to promote these behaviors during team meetings?

1. _____

2. _____

3. _____

4. _____

5. _____

6. _____

Tool 4.6: Quick check

Directions: After each meeting, look at your list of your team's basic ground rules and take a minute to consider whether team members followed them. You may use the suggestions below to add to the ground rules your team has set.

- ❏ Did every member join in the team's discussions?

- ❏ Did each member listen attentively as others spoke?

- ❏ Did one or two members dominate the discussions?

- ❏ Did all members arrive on time and stay for the entire meeting?

- ❏ Were all members prepared for the meeting when they arrived?

- ❏ Were all members "totally present" during the meeting?

- ❏ Did each member of the group believe that his or her time at the meeting was well spent?

WHAT WE DID WELL

_____

_____

_____

_____

_____

_____

_____

_____

WHAT WE WILL IMPROVE

_____

_____

_____

_____

_____

_____

_____

_____

Source: "A simple test can be revealing," by Joan Richardson. (1999, August/September.) *Tools for Schools*, 8.

Tool 4.7: Norms tune-up

Directions: If team meetings need some smoothing, revisit the norms set during earlier meetings. Have chart paper available to record any new procedures and ground rules on which the team reaches consensus. The leader for this meeting can use these questions to guide the discussion or can let each member write individual responses before a general discussion.

1. What norms do we usually observe well?

    _____

    _____

    _____

    _____

2. Which norms do we seem to ignore?

    _____

    _____

    _____

    _____

3. What behaviors are team members using now that seem to be useful?

    _____

    _____

    _____

    _____

4. What behaviors surprise us or make us uneasy?

    _____

    _____

    _____

    _____

5. Based on our answers to these questions, what norms do we now need? List new and adjusted norms below.

    _____

    _____

    _____

    _____

Tool 4.8: A brainstorming protocol

Directions: Brainstorming is a way of generating an assortment of ideas without criticism or judgment regarding the quality of those ideas. The team leader, or another team member, can use this procedure to lead team members to brainstorm answers to questions or responses to issues as needed.

1. Have chart paper and markers available.

2. Write the question or issue the team is addressing at the top of the chart paper.

3. Explain the following guidelines for generating responses to the question or issue:
    *   Ideas should be developed as fast as possible.
    *   Everyone on the team should contribute ideas.
    *   Unique and off-the-wall ideas are welcome.
    *   Do not critique or evaluate ideas during the brainstorming period.
    *   No discussion during this time! Just throw out ideas.

4. Begin with the first question or issue the team will address and toss out ideas. List all suggestions on the chart paper. Continue until the supply of ideas seems exhausted.

5. Examine team members' suggestions. Team members may now explain their ideas or ask questions about ideas that others suggested. They should delve more deeply into each other's thinking and consider which ideas are most useful.

6. With a marker, put a check mark by keepers — those suggestions that all team members agree to include as one of the answers for the question or issue.

7. Cross out ideas that team members do not think work well as a response.

8. Reach consensus on remaining suggestions, and decide whether or not to include them with the team's list of agreed-upon responses.

9. Compile a list of all keepers.

10. Continue using this process as needed to generate a list of ideas for each question or issue the team needs to discuss.

Tool 4.9: Tips for team members

Directions: Reproduce this page as a chart or poster to help learning team members keep in mind tips for building a successful team.

Tips for team members

1. Become a quick-change artist. Keep an open mind to new ideas.

2. Add value. Scope out opportunities to contribute and be responsible.

3. Take ownership for yourself and the team. Learn about the professional learning team process. Take initiative and responsibility.

4. Become a lifelong learner. Study, research, and educate yourself.

5. Manage your own morale. Keep a positive attitude.

6. Ask for what you need. This includes information, resources, materials, assistance, training, and support.

Source: *Team Member's Survival Guide,* by Jill George and Jeanne Wilson. New York: McGraw-Hill, 1997.

Tool 5.1: What *are* data?

Directions: Teams thinking about improving teaching and learning can find a lot more information than just grades and test results. Data-driven schools in Alabama used these data sources in their school improvement process. Review the list, then brainstorm what other data may be available. Determine as a team which sources you want to use.

STATE & NATIONAL TEST RESULTS
- State-mandated subject-area assessments
- Writing assessments
- Graduation exams
- College entrance exams
- Advanced placement exams
- Yearly progress reports
- National Assessment of Educational Progress scores

COMMERCIAL ASSESSMENTS
- Packaged program assessments
- Individual reading assessments

CLASSROOM ASSESSMENTS
- Daily and unit tests
- Student portfolios
- Checklists
- Running records
- Evaluations of student projects
- Evaluations of student performances
- Examples of student work

SURVEYS
- Student
- Parent
- Community
- Uncertified staff
- Targeted teacher surveys by grade level and content area (program effectiveness, staff development needs, technology, library, paperwork, duties, etc.)

SCHOOL CLIMATE
- Attendance records
- Counseling referrals
- Discipline reports (with trend analysis)
- Student comments to counselors, teachers

SCHOOLWIDE ASSESSMENTS
- School report cards
- School Improvement Plan yearly assessments
- Collective analyses of student work
- Schoolwide writing assessments
- Products of accreditation processes
- Reports from school walk-throughs

OTHER STUDENT DATA
- Course assignments
- College admission data
- Quarterly, interim, and final grades
- Dropout data
- Minutes/records of student support teams
- Special education referrals

OTHER DATA
- Student honors and awards
- Student and parent demographic information
- Results of teacher action research
- Reports from teachers
- Academic lab and library usage
- Faculty turnover rate
- Registration data

Source: Compiled by John Norton for the Alabama Best Practices Center.

Tool 5.2a: Subgroup analysis chart

Directions: Fill in this chart as completely as possible using the records you have to analyze student data by subgroups. A completed sample is included as a reference if you need it.

SUBGROUP TO BE ANALYZED (e.g. race, gender, other demographics) _____					
Categories within this subgroup					
Percent of students in each category					
Content area to be examined					
Results/scores/ performance for each subgroup					
Strengths *What are the strongest areas for this subgroup?*					
Weaknesses *What are the weakest areas for this subgroup?*					
Patterns and trends *What patterns and trends are striking?*					
Change from previous years *Is this a consistent trend?*					
Consistency across grade levels *Is this trend similar in all grades?*					
Consistency across subject areas *Is this trend evident in all subjects?*					

Tool 5.2b: Sample subgroup analysis chart

Directions: Refer to this completed chart as an example of a subgroup analysis chart examining similarities and differences among students of different ethnicities. You might similarly examine data for gender, exceptional children, socioeconomic levels, and other categories of students in your school.

SUBGROUP TO BE ANALYZED (e.g. race, gender, other demographics)					
Ethnicity					
Categories within this subgroup	African-American	American Indian	Asian	Caucasian	Hispanic
Percent of students in each category	36%	3%	4%	43%	14%
Content area to be examined	Reading				
Results/scores/ performance for each subgroup	44.6% proficient	52.3% proficient	69.4% proficient	58.8% proficient	51.2% proficient
Strengths *What are the strongest areas for this subgroup?*	Main ideas Significant details	Main ideas Significant details	Main ideas Significant details Vocabulary	Main ideas Vocabulary Significant details	Main ideas Significant details
Weaknesses *What are the weakest areas for this subgroup?*	Inference Comparisons Vocabulary	Inference Cause-effect Summarizing	Inference Cause-effect	Inference Comparisons Summarizing	Inference Vocabulary Cause-effect
Patterns and trends *What patterns and trends are striking?*	Student reading comprehension is lower than we want in all categories. Inference, cause-and-effect, comparison, summarizing, and vocabulary are the most critical areas of focus.				
Change from previous years *Is this a consistent trend?*	Some improvement	N/A	Consistent trend	Some improvement	Some improvement
Consistency across grade levels *Is this trend similar in all grades?*	Yes	Yes	Yes	Yes	Yes
Consistency across subject areas *Is this trend evident in all subjects?*	Similar across subject areas	Math scores typically lower	Math scores typically higher	Math scores typically lower	Math scores typically lower

Tool 5.3: Reflecting on the data

Directions: Think about what you learned from examining student information and data, and write your responses to the questions. Discuss your answers with your team. Have a recorder make notes of big ideas and decisions from this discussion.

What sources of data did we examine?

_____

_____

What parts of these data really caught our attention?

_____

_____

What parts of these data encourage you the most?

_____

_____

What parts concern you the most?

_____

_____

What differences, if any, are there in grades, attendance, and behavior among our students?

_____

_____

Do some groups of students achieve at higher levels than others? If so, to what degree?

_____

_____

Which students are not working to potential? What evidence is there that students who were given more challenging work also achieved more?

_____

_____

Which groups appear to need instruction more tailored to their learning styles?

_____

_____

What other questions does this data raise for you?

_____

_____

What are the implications for what our professional learning team should focus on this year?

_____

_____

Tool 5.4: Deciding on a team focus

Directions: What is your team's instructional focus for the year? Discuss and record this decision after analyzing and reflecting on student and subgroup data. This information will be used to help you craft your team goal.

What student strengths do these data highlight?

_____

_____

What student needs do these data highlight?

_____

_____

What are the implications of the data we examined for our professional learning team?

_____

_____

On what areas could we focus our collective efforts? What are the pros and cons of each?

_____

_____

Which area will we select as an intensive focus for our team's work?

_____

_____

What results do we want for our students by the end of the school year?

_____

_____

TEAM FOCUS: General area of student need we will address

_____

_____

_____

Tool 5.5a: Decision-making cycle for developing goals

Directions: Use this diagram as a poster or team visual to keep you on track in thinking about goals. Remember that all team members must completely understand and agree on the goal.

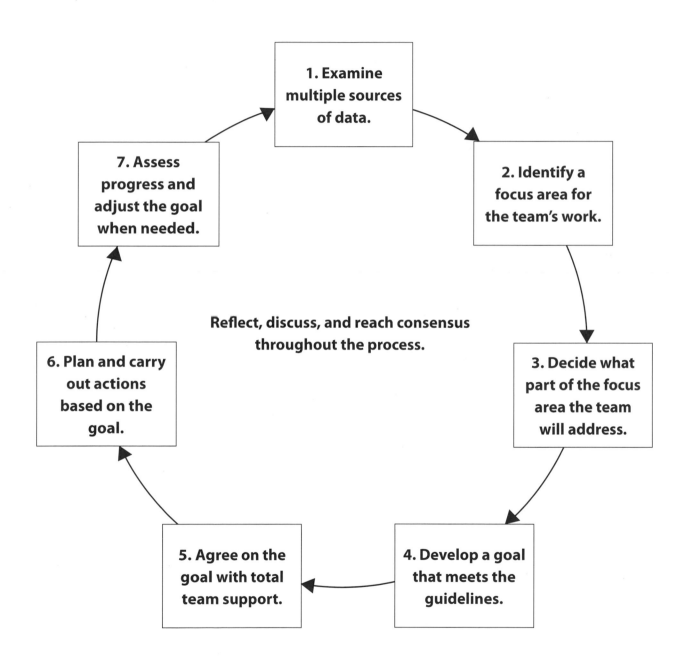

1. Examine multiple sources of data.

2. Identify a focus area for the team's work.

3. Decide what part of the focus area the team will address.

4. Develop a goal that meets the guidelines.

5. Agree on the goal with total team support.

6. Plan and carry out actions based on the goal.

7. Assess progress and adjust the goal when needed.

Reflect, discuss, and reach consensus throughout the process.

Tool 5.5b: Decision-making cycle description

Directions: Clarify stages of the decision-making cycle by elaborating as a team on actions and ideas you think are included in Stage 1. Then read the information below and add that information to your understanding. Use this procedure to examine each stage.

Stage 1: Examine multiple sources of data. Study at least three sources of data about students. If you think of data as test scores or report card grades, you will ignore many characteristics of good learners — initiative, creativity, conceptual thinking, judgment, special talents, and more.

Stage 2: Identify a focus area for the team's work. The data will reveal areas of relative strength and weakness in student achievement in different categories and probably among subgroups. This information can suggest an area on which to concentrate your efforts.

Stage 3: Decide what part of the focus area the team will address. Your team's work will target an area in which students need help to learn and achieve at higher levels. Team members may develop a goal that encompasses a broad area of need or may home in on a part of that area. For example, if your team focus is reading comprehension, you might set an initial goal dealing with that general area and then narrow your goal as teachers diagnose specific reading difficulties that call for more specific interventions.

Stage 4: Develop a goal that meets the guidelines. Tools 5.6 to 5.8 offer guidelines for developing a goal that will set a concrete direction for the team. In addition to being based on student learning needs, your goal needs to be clear, collaboratively developed, measurable, and realistic. It should focus on teacher learning and actions that will increase student achievement.

Stage 5: Agree on the goal with total team support. All team members should agree on the team goal. Without understanding the goal and/or believing that the goal is valuable to them, members may unintentionally sabotage the team's efforts. Tool 10.11 may help team members reach agreement if necessary.

Stage 6: Plan and carry out actions based on the goal. The goal should propel team members into learning and action and keep members focused on the purpose of this professional learning team.

Stage 7: Assess progress and adjust the goal when needed. As team members increase their knowledge and learn more about students' challenges, the work may become more targeted and the team goal should reflect that shift. Keeping the goal tightly focused keeps the team more focused and leads to more purposeful and productive team meetings.

Tool 5.6: Team goal-setting guidelines

Directions: You know from your data analysis on what general area you will focus your efforts. Now set a goal to propel you on your way. Read these guidelines in your group and ask each member to be responsible for keeping one or two in the discussion as you establish your goal.

MAKE YOUR GOAL:

- **Clear.** The team goal is totally clear and completely understood by each team member. Every member should understand and be able to explain what the team intends to achieve.

- **Needs-based.** The goal results from a data analysis and addresses an area in which students need to learn and achieve at higher levels. The goal states how teachers will increase their effectiveness as professionals so students benefit.

- **Shared.** The goal has value and commitment from everyone on the team. When all team members work together toward a common goal, one's success contributes to the success of all. Collaboration builds synergy and good working relationships.

- **Measurable.** Team members need to see the results of their efforts and to get feedback about progress toward their goals. The team needs ways to measure the progress and to determine to what extent the goal is being achieved.

- **Doable.** The goal is realistic and achievable within a specified time frame. Generally, that time frame is the school year. Do not aim low, but do not overreach or the team may become discouraged by a lack of perceived progress. Take on a manageable challenge.

Be sure to write down your goal!

Tool 5.7: Setting your team goal

Directions: This tool provides information for setting team goals. Read this information silently, then discuss the sample goals with your teammates and work together to draft a team goal.

Professional learning team goals focus on **teacher growth.** Team members will work together all year toward personal and professional growth targeting an area of student need.

A professional learning team goal may be written as a question:

- What research-based practices can we use in our classrooms to help all of our students better understand what they read in their textbooks?
- What can we do differently in our classrooms to improve student achievement in math computation across all grade levels?

A learning team goal may be written as a purpose statement:

- We will gain knowledge and skill in using inquiry-based methods of teaching science to engage students in higher levels of thinking and learning.
- We will increase our knowledge and skill in using number talks to identify student knowledge gaps and misconceptions, and to create effective cross grade-level teaching practices for overcoming these.

DISCUSS AND DECIDE:

1. Consider your students. In what areas do they need your help? What will your general focus be?

_____

_____

_____

2. Consider yourselves. What do you all need to learn and be able to do more effectively to meet these students' needs in this area?

_____

_____

_____

3. Write a goal for your team. Refer to Tools 5.5 and 5.6 as you develop this goal.

_____

_____

_____

4. Check out your goal using Tool 5.8.

Tool 5.8: Check out that goal

Directions: Discuss the answers to these questions about your goal statement with your learning team. If your team cannot answer yes to the first seven questions, decide how to rewrite your goal statement to bring it in line with the guidelines for a clear goal.

1. Is the goal clearly stated?   ___Yes ___No

2. Does it focus on teacher learning?   ___Yes ___No

3. Does it focus on teachers becoming more accomplished in instruction? ___Yes ___No

4. Does it focus on a specific area?   ___Yes ___No

5. Do students need help in this area?   ___Yes ___No

6. Do all team members agree on this goal?   ___Yes ___No

7. Is it doable?   ___Yes ___No

8. How will you be able to tell that your team is making progress?

_____

_____

_____

_____

_____

Tool 6.1: Reflect on our beliefs and assumptions

Directions: What assumptions about teaching and learning drive your instruction and that of your team members? Write your team's goal in the top box. Then reflect on your personal answers for these questions and make notes in the spaces provided. Following personal reflection, discuss each question as a team. The team recorder should compile a list of team members' thoughts and responses and have these available as the team drafts a plan.

TEAM GOAL:	
1. What specific needs do our students have in this area?	
2. What do we believe high-quality teaching in this area looks like? What would teachers and students be doing?	
3. What do our current instructional practices look like in this area?	
4. What do our current practices imply about how we believe our students learn?	
5. What beliefs about our students do we want our teaching to reflect?	
6. Is there a gap between what we believe about teaching and learning and what we actually do? If so, why?	

Tool 6.2: Reflect on our current reality

Directions: Write your thoughts about each question, then work with others on your team to make decisions. These questions can help guide your team in developing a relevant and rigorous plan for reaching your goal. If brainstorming would be helpful, use Tool 4.8.

TEAM GOAL:	
1. What knowledge and experience do we already have in this area?	
2. What do we as team members need to understand at a deeper level to be able to increase student learning in this area?	
3. What instructional practices are we already using that would have a greater impact on student learning if we improved them?	
4. What new instructional practices can we adopt that would help our students learn and achieve at higher levels?	

Source: The Mobile Math Initiative (MMI) and Susan Pruet.

5. Specifically, what professional learning and instructional growth do we want to achieve this year?	
6. How will we know we are becoming more accomplished in our teaching? What information might we gather to determine whether we are succeeding?	
7. What resources and assistance will we need to carry out our plans?	
8. How will we communicate to others information about what we are learning and doing?	

Source: The Mobile Math Initiative (MMI) and Susan Pruet.

Tool 6.3: Reflect on priorities and actions

Directions: Brainstorm and discuss responses to these questions, and reach consensus. Take time to discuss ideas and get input from everyone on the team.

TEAM GOAL :	
1. What will we explore, learn, and plan to do in order to reach our goal?	
2. What activities might we engage in as we work toward our goal?	
3. What should our main activities and tasks be in the first month?	
4. What kind of timeline would we propose for the remaining activities and tasks?	

Tool 6.4: Team long-term planning guide

Directions: After discussing, reflecting, and making notes about issues from Tools 2.1, 6.2, and 6.3, begin to develop a plan. This plan will likely change as the team continues to meet and learn together, so think in terms of a monthly plan until all feel ready to develop a long-term plan.

Decide as a team on milestones for the month, and then work together to determine activities, resources, and responsibilities to accomplish these milestones. Be certain that activities you select focus on teacher learning and growth.

Team goal: _____

Milestones: What we plan to achieve this month through our professional learning team work.

Achievement area	Milestones/accomplishments *(Keep realistic and achievable)*	By when?
For students		
For teachers		
For our learning team		

Activities: What we plan to do to help us achieve our milestones and move toward our goal:

Activity	Tasks to complete activity	Person(s) responsible

Resources: Books, materials, and other resources we will need.

_____

_____

Additional plans:

_____

_____

_____

_____

_____

_____

_____

_____

_____

Tool 6.5: Plan for team growth

Directions: Begin now to plan for success as a productive team. Use this tool to track how well your team is modeling these 10 important characteristics. Discuss each characteristic together, and fill in the column at right. Complete a chart at regular intervals — monthly or quarterly.

Date _____

TEAM GROWTH INDICATORS	What might someone observing us see or hear that would indicate we're growing in this direction?
Maintain a focus on teacher professional growth.	
Abide by norms that guide team interactions and behaviors.	
Learn new and relevant information about teaching.	
Share leadership and responsibility.	
Communicate to others what we are learning and doing.	
Meet regularly and on schedule.	
Practice trusting behaviors.	
Work productively as a team.	
Apply new knowledge and skills in the classroom.	
Monitor student learning and success.	

Tool 7.1: Let's get acquainted!

Directions: Please prepare to share some information about yourself with your teammates. Answer the questions below. Use the back of the paper if you need more space. Bring this sheet with you to our professional learning team meeting.

Name_____

E-mail address_____

Teaching assignment _____

1. Interests and hobbies:

    _____

    _____

    _____

2. Information about your family:

    _____

    _____

    _____

3. Something you look forward to about teaching:

    _____

    _____

    _____

4. Something that troubles you about teaching:

    _____

    _____

    _____

5. Something you want to learn about teaching:

    _____

    _____

    _____

6. What you like best about your students:

    _____

    _____

    _____

7. Your chief concern for your students:

    _____

    _____

    _____

8. Something you've accomplished:

    _____

    _____

    _____

9. Something you plan to accomplish:

    _____

    _____

    _____

10. Something else about you:

    _____

    _____

    _____

Tool 7.5: The dysfunctional discussion division

Directions: Pretend you are assembling a team of individuals whose assignment is to shut down productive conversation on your team. Pick from this group, or recruit your own dysfunctional disruptors and name those persons.

The Abrupt Advisor. Assignment: To offer immediate advice without active listening or working through issues. *("What we can do is…")*

The Circuitous Communicator. Assignment: To communicate indirectly with a team member through someone else. *("I don't think she's right about…")*

The Intimidator. Assignment: To verbally bully others with the intention of harming their ideas and suggestions. *("That's the most ridiculous thing I ever heard.")*

The Judge. Assignment: To place blame or make judgments about team members. Often involves finger pointing. *("What you said isn't true…")*

The Mind Reader. Assignment: To assume that he or she can read other team members minds, even on confusing issues. *("I already know what you're getting at…")*

The Know-It-All. Assignment: To circumvent discussion by assuring others that there's no need to talk because he or she already knows what should be done. *("I've done this many times.")*

The Mixed-Message Expert. Assignment: To send a message where the words say one thing, but the body language or attitude convey a different meaning.

The Naysayer. Assignment: To cast gloom and doom on other team members' suggestions. *("That won't work.")*

The Parent Substitute. Assignment: To give people advice. *("You should do this…")*

The Patronizer. Assignment: To discount or minimize another person's comments by inappropriate and excessive reassuring or humoring. *("Oh come now, you know better than…")*

The Silent Accuser. Assignment: To silently nurture feelings of resentment or anger and withdraw.

The Terminator. Assignment: To deliver statements that shut down or cut off discussion with no opening to continue. *("We already know that.")*

The Whine Wizard. Assignment: To complain at every opportunity. *("Why do we have to…?")*

Now assemble a team to counter those discussion destructors. Work with others in your group to develop a Creative Communicators Corps. What types of individuals would you pick?

Tool 7.6a: Trust factors

Directions: The characteristics below help to increase trust among team members. Build a picture of the trust level in your team by placing marks on the chart (Tool 7.6b) at the appropriate level for each trust factor. Consider your team members as a whole when indicating the level of trust.

- **Care:** We care about each other professionally and personally, and we are willing to go the extra mile for one another. We show sensitivity to one another's needs, desires, and interests.

- **Collaboration:** We limit our competitive tendencies to lower the barriers between us. We share power and control during the course of our work rather than hoarding it.

- **Competence:** We believe in each other's ability and willingness to fulfill our responsibilities effectively. We believe that everyone on our team has skills and is capable of contributing.

- **Confidence:** We have confidence in one another, and we lean on one another. We believe we will all fulfill our obligations and do the right thing for the right reasons.

- **Consistency:** We behave in consistent and predictable ways. Our words match our subsequent actions, and we honor our team commitments. We do what we say we will do.

- **Integrity:** We trust each other to put the interests of students first and to make changes to meet their needs. We are clear about the intentions and motives for others' actions.

- **Openness:** We communicate accurately, openly, and transparently. We lay our cards on the table respectfully, and others accept who we are and what we think.

- **Conviviality:** Our team meeting atmosphere is relaxed and enjoyable. People can be direct in their communications.

- **Respect:** We acknowledge one another's ideas and interact in courteous ways. We genuinely listen to one another and treat each other with dignity.

- **Self-acceptance:** We are comfortable with ourselves. We accept ourselves and our potential.

- **Support:** We verbally and publicly support each other.

- **Familiarity:** We get to know each other. We know each other's interests, contributions, abilities. We are aware and accepting of team members' assets and shortcomings.

STAGE OF CONCERN	HOW TEAM MEMBERS FEEL AND THINK AT EACH LEVEL	EXAMPLES OF INTERVENTIONS
AWARENESS	I have little information, concern, or involvement with professional learning teams. I am not concerned about this change and am not doing anything about it.	• Web resources and written resources about professional learning teams. • Opportunities to attend workshops and conferences. • Conversations providing a rationale for professional learning teams.
INFORMATIONAL	I have a general interest in professional learning teams and would like to know more about this process. I'm taking the initiative to learn more about learning teams.	• Question-and-answer sessions. • Discussions with individuals who have expertise with professional learning teams via conferences or webinars. • Opportunities to attend workshops and conferences.
PERSONAL	I want to know the personal impact of the professional learning team initiative.	• Information about time and work commitments. • Involvement in planning for learning teams. • Discussions with experts in professional learning teams. • Facilitated discussions.
MANAGEMENT	I am concerned about how professional learning teams will be managed in practice and what members need to know in order to do this work.	• Organizing and planning sessions. • Information on logistics and debriefings. • Involvement in planning for professional learning teams. • Training in learning team work.
CONSEQUENCE	I want to know how my work in a professional learning team affects my colleagues and my students, and how to make my involvement have more impact. I am moving from simply attending meetings to making changes to improve teaching and learning.	• Surveys. • Self-assessments. • Reflection. • Experimentation. • Communication with other learning teams. • Assistance with diagnostic activities such as looking at student work. • Access to research and study materials.
COLLABORATION	I share, coordinate, and align my professional growth and teaching practices with others on my team. I depend on them, and I give them help and support. I have joined forces with other teachers to have a collective impact on teaching and learning.	• More frequent opportunities to share, coordinate, and learn with colleagues. • Opportunities to observe colleagues. • Schoolwide information sharing about learning teams. • Communication and interaction with other professional learning teams. • Opportunities to share at conferences.
REFOCUSING	I am interested in making our professional learning team even more effective, and I have ideas about modifications that might work even better.	• Review of research on professional learning teams. • Field-testing of products from professional learning team work. • Data analysis. • Consistent and regular support.

Source: *Implementing Change: Patterns, Principles, and Potholes,* 2nd edition, by Gene E. Hall and Shirley M. Hord. Boston: Allyn & Bacon, 2005.

Tool 8.2 Levels of Use

Directions: The Concerns-Based Adoption Model (CBAM), a well-researched model from the Southwest Educational Development Laboratory, identifies eight Levels of Use that describe how teachers act or behave as they adopt a new program or initiative.

Use the chart on the next page to identify where you fall in the Levels of Use of this new initiative. Discuss with your colleagues where they feel they are, and determine what assistance your team may want so members are able to move to the next stage.

Examples of interventions have been added as ideas that can help you progress through the levels.

LEVELS OF USE	WHAT TEAM MEMBERS DO AT EACH LEVEL	EXAMPLES OF INTERVENTIONS
Nonuse	Team members demonstrate no interest, no involvement, or are taking no action.	• Written information and web resources. • Overviews and displays. • Explanation of the rationale for professional learning teams. • Personal contacts with knowledgeable users.
Orientation	Team members express a general interest in professional learning teams, would like to know more, and are taking the initiative to learn more about the professional learning team process.	• Workshops. • Question-and-answer sessions. • Discussions with facilitators. • Talks with experienced team members.
Preparation	Team members are making definite plans to begin participating in professional learning teams and are learning the processes and skills needed to successfully implement this initiative.	• Guided overview of tools and materials. • Advice and tools for learning team management. • Modeling and practice with teaming strategies. • Consensus on area for team focus.
Mechanical	Team members are attempting to organize and master the tasks required in the early stages of implementation. The focus is mainly on day-to-day use of learning teams with little reflection.	• Study and research to deepen content knowledge in a focus area. • Use of norms to smooth bumps. • Regular self-assessments by team members of their teamwork. • Logistical help and support.
Routine	Team members are making few or no changes and have an established, comfortable pattern of working in a professional learning team. Little preparation or thought is being given to improving the use of learning teams.	• Study and research to deepen content knowledge in the focus area. • Application of learning to the classroom. • Examination of student work. • Development and use of formative assessments.
Refinement	Team members are making changes to increase the impact and consequences of professional learning teams.	• Study and research to deepen content knowledge in the focus area. • Development and use of joint instructional strategies. • Observations of colleagues who are using strategies. • Examination of student work. • Use of formative assessments.
Integration	Team members are working deliberately to coordinate and combine efforts with others using professional learning teams in order to have a collective impact.	• Professional learning team activities and information shared schoolwide. • Learning teams used as a vehicle for collaborative mentoring. • Work with colleagues to develop joint instructional practices.
Renewal	Team members reevaluate professional learning teams and seek ways to make them increasingly effective in order to achieve greater impact.	• Data analysis. • Review of new information and research. • Field testing of new instructional products. • Consistent and regular support.

Source: *Implementing Change: Patterns, Principles, and Potholes,* 2nd edition, by Gene E. Hall and Shirley M. Hord. Boston: Allyn & Bacon, 2005.

Tool 8.3: Tool talk

Directions: Choose a tool that you feel best represents the group's work so far. You may also choose a tool not represented here. Tell the group why you selected the tool you did and how it represents the team's work. Share a hope or expectation you have for future meetings.

Tool 8.6: Feedback analysis

Directions: Use this tool to give suggestions concerning my feedback on your professional learning team work. Check the box that best matches your response to each question and offer suggestions. You may remain anonymous.

What I, as the facilitator, need to know about the feedback I provide	Yes	At times	No	What should I continue doing? How can I improve?
1. Is the feedback specific to the needs of your professional learning team?				
2. Is the feedback clear? Do you understand?				
3. Is the feedback consistent? Does it help you maintain a steady direction in your professional learning team?				
4. Is the feedback positive? Does it acknowledge your team's good performance?				
5. Is the feedback frequent and timely?				
6. Does the feedback seem critical or negative?				
7. Does the feedback provide you with useful support?				
8. Is the feedback constructive? Does it help you understand how your team is doing?				
9. Is the feedback upbeat when it is public? Does it contribute to a risk-free professional learning team environment?				
10. Does the feedback provide you with information you need to find your own solutions?				
11. Does the feedback give you more information than you can use about issues?				
12. Does the feedback overload you with suggestions and advice?				
13. Does the feedback indicate support for your learning team and caring about your success?				
14. Does the feedback acknowledge your professional learning team's accomplishments?				
15. Do you feel that the feedback is sincerely and honestly intended to help your team?				
16. Is it OK to continue to provide you with feedback on meetings and other professional learning team issues?				

Tool 8.7: It's OK! cards — teacher version

Directions: Copy and cut apart the cards. Give each team member a card to remind him or her that learning comes as much from our successes as from our failures. This ticket gives team members permission to try a new strategy, fail, and try again. It also entitles them to support from you and their colleagues.

- **Web sites.** Many educational organization web sites offer a rich supply of information in a variety of subject areas and topics. The starter list below may help generate ideas and link teachers to some current research and cutting-edge instructional practices.

  - **Access Excellence @ the National Health Museum** (www.accessexcellence.org/) is a highly interactive site that provides an array of free, cutting-edge resources for health, life science, biology, and other bioscience teachers.

  - **The National Council for the Social Studies** web site provides free lesson plans for download at www.socialstudies.org/lessons/ and teaching resources at www.socialstudies.org/resources/.

  - **The National Science Digital Library (NSDL) Middle School Portal,** http://msteacher.org/default.aspx. This site is a direct path to online resources for instruction and professional development. You can click on the links to access the math pathway (http://msteacher.org/math.aspx) to locate resources to help teachers and students thoroughly explore teaching and learning in mathematics. A companion site (http://msteacher.org/science.aspx) offers resources and links for science.

  - **ReadWriteThink** (www.readwritethink.org/) is the site of the International Reading Association and the National Council of Teachers of English. This site provides teachers and students access to high-quality practices and resources in reading and language arts instruction.

  - **Thinkfinity** (www.marcopolo-education.org/home.aspx), a web site linking literacy, education, and technology, provides standards-based resources, including lesson plans, student materials, reviewed Internet resources, and interactive resources.

Tool 8.12: Database of teacher talent

Directions: Please give us some information on your professional skills and interests. No modesty allowed! Responses will help identify specific expertise, teaching strategies, and interests so faculty members know whom to call if they need a consultant or peer coach in a particular area.

Name	
Teaching assignment	
Effective teaching strategies you use	
Professional development events you've attended	
Presentations you have made	
Other professional interests	
Other professional activities	
Additional information about you	

Tool 8.13: Hunting for help

Directions: Fill in the answers to each question to help identify teachers and others who can assist teams with specific topics. Place the form in teachers' boxes, post it on the faculty or professional learning team bulletin board, post it on a school wiki, or e-mail it to faculty members.

Our professional learning team is working on this topic:

_____
_____
_____
_____
_____
_____

We are looking for fresh ideas and expertise in this area:

_____
_____
_____
_____
_____
_____

Please contact us or write your name below if you are willing to talk with us or act as a resource for us.

Thanks!

_____

(E-mail, phone, or other contact information)

Tool 8.14: Share a site

Directions: List your favorite education web sites, and give some information about them.

Web site name:	Web address:
What's it about?	**Why do you like it?**

Web site name:	Web address:
What's it about?	**Why do you like it?**

Web site name:	Web address:
What's it about?	**Why do you like it?**

Tool 9.1: Participant perception survey

Directions: Rate your perceptions of this professional learning team event by circling your response to each question on this short survey. The highest rating is 5 (totally met my need) and the lowest is 1 (did not help at all). NA means that this issue was not addressed.

TO WHAT EXTENT DID THIS EVENT:	Low			High		
1. Increase your understanding of the rationale for professional learning teams?	1	2	3	4	5	NA
2. Clarify the difference between professional learning teams and other types of team meetings?	1	2	3	4	5	NA
3. Help you with preliminary logistics and organizing for professional learning teams?	1	2	3	4	5	NA
4. Explain the reason and a process for setting team norms?	1	2	3	4	5	NA
5. Guide you in beginning a planning process?	1	2	3	4	5	NA
6. Provide ideas for conducting successful team meetings?	1	2	3	4	5	NA
7. Offer useful information for building interpersonal skills?	1	2	3	4	5	NA
8. Suggest ways to build an effective team communication process?	1	2	3	4	5	NA
9. Provide workable ideas to help maintain team momentum?	1	2	3	4	5	NA
10. Provide tools and information for assessing team progress?	1	2	3	4	5	NA
11. Actively engage you in the learning process?	1	2	3	4	5	NA
12. Allow you to interact and work with other participants?	1	2	3	4	5	NA
13. Give you useful tools for working in professional learning teams?	1	2	3	4	5	NA
14. Provide you with new insight?	1	2	3	4	5	NA
15. Increase your interest in being a member of a professional learning team?	1	2	3	4	5	NA
16. Lead you to feel that your time attending this event was well spent?	1	2	3	4	5	NA

Is there additional information that you would like to have? If so, what information?

Please share comments, ideas, and suggestions here or on the back of this survey.

_____

_____

_____

_____

_____

Tool 9.2: Pre/post survey

Directions: Use the following scale to rate each statement in terms of how well it describes your knowledge and feelings about teacher collaboration. Circle the number that best expresses your answer. Do not put your name or any identifying information on this survey.

	Strongly disagree	Disagree	Agree	Strongly agree
1. I am familiar with the rationale for teachers collaborating on classroom instruction.	1	2	3	4
2. I know the basic procedures that make up structured learning team meetings.	1	2	3	4
3. I feel that meeting regularly in teams to focus on increasing teachers' knowledge and expertise would be valuable.	1	2	3	4
4. I prefer to work alone to learn and to increase my teaching expertise.	1	2	3	4
5. I prefer to participate in regular meetings with colleagues to learn and increase my teaching expertise.	1	2	3	4
6. When we work together on committees at this school, the atmosphere is collegial.	1	2	3	4
7. When teachers at my school work in groups, all members participate and share responsibilities.	1	2	3	4
8. I regularly read professional journals and current research on teaching and learning.	1	2	3	4
9. I regularly look for different teaching strategies and adjust or change my teaching practices throughout the year.	1	2	3	4
10. I want to learn and practice new ways to teach.	1	2	3	4

Tool 9.3: Survey of teacher beliefs about teaming

Directions: Answer each question thoughtfully and honestly. This information will be used to plan the professional learning team process that will be most valuable to you. Do not put your name on this survey or include identifying information.

1. How much experience have you had with collaborative teamwork for learning?

    _____

    _____

    _____

    _____

2. How often do you call on fellow teachers for help with teaching ideas and strategies?

    _____

    _____

    _____

    _____

3. How important is it to you to work together with other teachers?

    _____

    _____

    _____

    _____

4. What benefits do you expect to gain from working in professional learning teams?

    _____

    _____

    _____

    _____

5. What disadvantages do you perceive to working in a professional learning team?

    _____

    _____

    _____

    _____

Tool 9.4: Year one debriefing questions

Directions: Answer each question thoughtfully and honestly. This information will be used to improve the professional learning team process. Do not put your name on this survey or include identifying information.

THINKING ABOUT THE PROFESSIONAL LEARNING TEAM PROCESS

1. What part of the process do you feel has been most successful? Why?

   _____

   _____

2. What part of the process do you feel has been least successful? Why?

   _____

   _____

3. What part of the learning team procedure needs to be adjusted? How would you change it?

   _____

   _____

4. What additional support would you like to have?

   _____

   _____

5. What would make learning teams more valuable for teachers?

   _____

   _____

6. What changes have occurred as a result of working together in learning teams? (Individual, team, classroom, students, school)

   _____

   _____

7. What would you like to see happen in professional learning teams in the future?

   _____

   _____

8. Use the back of this page to make additional comments.

Tool 9.5: Year two planning questions

Directions for teams: Use this tool to help you plan and set directions at the beginning of the second year of professional learning teams. Add questions and information as needed to help you examine the work your team did last year and get ready for planning a course of action this year.

1. What are some indicators that our team made progress last year?

   _____

   _____

2. What new information did we learn that improved our teaching?

   _____

   _____

3. What new teaching practices did we use in our classrooms as a result of our professional learning team work?

   _____

   _____

4. What evidence do we have that these practices did/did not work?

   _____

   _____

5. Do we think our time in professional learning team meetings this year will be well-spent? Why or why not?

   _____

   _____

6. What will make our professional learning team experience more valuable this year?

   _____

   _____

7. What happened because of our professional learning team that probably would not otherwise have happened?

   _____

   _____

8. What do we want our team to accomplish by the end of this school year?

   _____

   _____

Tool 9.8: Professional learning team survey

Directions: Give your opinions about your professional learning team. There are no right or wrong responses. Do not put your name on this survey.

School _____ Subject/Grade level _____

1. How many times have you met with your learning team? _____ 1-7 _____ 8-14 _____ 15+ _____ Have not met
2. How many people are in your learning team? _____
3. On a scale of 1 to 10 (with 10 being the most positive), what rating best describes your feelings about these meetings?

Most negative (-)	1	2	3	4	5	6	7	8	9	10	Most positive (+)
Unproductive											Productive
Not task-oriented											Task-oriented
Not well-facilitated											Well-facilitated
Incompatible group members											Compatible group members
Less-than-honest communications											Honest communications

4. What, if any, are the positive effects of these meetings on you personally?

_____

_____

5. What, if any, negative effects or concerns have you experienced with the learning team meetings?

_____

_____

6. Rate the extent to which you feel you have benefited by participating on a learning team.

Rating scale: 1 (not at all) to 5 (a great deal)

To what extent have you gained:	(Circle choice)
Research-based knowledge about teaching and learning?	1 2 3 4 5
Insights about how to reach certain students?	1 2 3 4 5
Ideas for increasing your teaching expertise?	1 2 3 4 5
Perspectives on your strengths and difficulties in teaching?	1 2 3 4 5
Greater understanding of ways to monitor results of teaching strategies and make adjustments?	1 2 3 4 5
Greater confidence in experimenting with a range of instructional methods?	1 2 3 4 5
A stronger sense of connection with and support from other team members?	1 2 3 4 5
A greater sense of yourself as a professional?	1 2 3 4 5

7. When thinking about your team's focus, how successful has your group been with each activity listed below?

Rating scale: 1 (not at all successful) to 5 (extremely successful)

How successful has your learning team been with:	(Circle choice)
Analyzing and discussing student needs?	1 2 3 4 5
Setting a long-term goal and purpose for your team's work?	1 2 3 4 5
Researching and studying successful teaching practices for addressing student needs, and discussing how to apply what you have read/studied?	1 2 3 4 5
Sharing successful teaching practices you currently use?	1 2 3 4 5
Investigating new instructional strategies and materials that might help students?	1 2 3 4 5
Working together to select and experiment with specific strategies in your classrooms?	1 2 3 4 5
Designing new materials, lessons, or assessments for students?	1 2 3 4 5
Trying out new materials and approaches in teaching and monitoring students' learning?	1 2 3 4 5
Looking at student work to diagnose student understandings and misconceptions?	1 2 3 4 5
Working as a productive team?	1 2 3 4 5
Developing collegial and caring working relationships?	1 2 3 4 5
Using logs to communicate with others (all faculty members, the principal, etc.) your team's work?	1 2 3 4 5

8. Below is a list of activities that support teacher growth and development. Choose and circle a rating based on your assessment of the extent to which the practice occurred (1) before learning teams were started and (2) at the conclusion of the first year of learning team meetings.

Rating scale: 1 (not very effectively practiced) to 5 (very effectively practiced)

	Before	After
Teachers talk to each other about teaching methods and results.	1 2 3 4 5	1 2 3 4 5
Teachers learn from each other by watching each other teach.	1 2 3 4 5	1 2 3 4 5
Teachers design lessons, assessments, and/or units together.	1 2 3 4 5	1 2 3 4 5
Teachers critique lessons, assessments, or units for each other.	1 2 3 4 5	1 2 3 4 5
Teachers develop strategies to address different types of learners.	1 2 3 4 5	1 2 3 4 5
Teachers share, read, and discuss articles, books, and other professional resources.	1 2 3 4 5	1 2 3 4 5
Teachers ask each other for advice and help with particular strategies or topics.	1 2 3 4 5	1 2 3 4 5
Teachers visit one another's classrooms to examine teaching strategies.	1 2 3 4 5	1 2 3 4 5
Teachers visit other schools to examine instructional approaches in different settings.	1 2 3 4 5	1 2 3 4 5
Teachers work together to examine student work samples to better understand student strengths and weaknesses.	1 2 3 4 5	1 2 3 4 5
Teachers provide moral support and encourage each other to try new ideas.	1 2 3 4 5	1 2 3 4 5
Teachers help each other implement new ideas and practices in the classroom.	1 2 3 4 5	1 2 3 4 5

9. In your opinion, what percent of the students whom you teach have benefited from your learning team participation?

      ___ less than 25%   ___ 26% to 50%   ___ 51% to 75%   ___ 76%+

10. Based on your experiences so far with the learning team:

Rating scale: 1 (not at all) to 5 (a great deal)

I think my participation on the learning team will:	*(Circle choice)*
Increase my overall teaching effectiveness.	1 2 3 4 5
Increase my skills in helping students learn.	1 2 3 4 5
Change my expectations for some students' learning abilities.	1 2 3 4 5
Increase my understanding of how to engage students in more rigorous learning.	1 2 3 4 5
Significantly change some of my teaching practices.	1 2 3 4 5
Significantly change ways in which I work with other teachers.	1 2 3 4 5

11. Rate the extent you agree or disagree with each of the following statements.

Rating scale: 1 (strongly disagree) to 5 (strongly agree)

I am enthusiastic about my participation on a learning team.	1 2 3 4 5
I feel a lot of stress during the work day.	1 2 3 4 5
I need more time to participate in my learning team.	1 2 3 4 5
The leadership here actively supports learning team participation.	1 2 3 4 5
I am excited by my students' accomplishments this year.	1 2 3 4 5
Student achievement is a major problem here.	1 2 3 4 5
My team has made progress in improving instructional practices this year.	1 2 3 4 5
Teachers here tend to work in isolation with little coordination.	1 2 3 4 5
The work environment here is collaborative and teachers get along well.	1 2 3 4 5
I often feel unsure of my teaching.	1 2 3 4 5
Learning teams are of value to teachers and students.	1 2 3 4 5

Source: SERVE Center at the University of North Carolina at Greensboro.

Tool 10.1: The facilitator's role

Directions: Use this tool to help you and other leaders understand roles and typical responsibilities of facilitators. You might use these suggestions to create a job description and responsibilities, to help leaders understand needed facilitation tasks, or to provide information when requesting funding for a professional learning team facilitator. This sheet also could be a checklist for you to determine your own strengths, keeping in mind that the list is not comprehensive and should be adapted for your situation. In areas you do not feel confident, locate someone to assist with that task while building your own skills.

THE PROFESSIONAL LEARNING TEAM FACILITATOR:

Models continual learning and builds knowledge and skill in the following areas:
- Professional learning team goals, concepts, and processes.
- Fundamentals of professional learning team work and of team development.
- Team facilitation strategies and skills.
- Working effectively with adult learners.
- Establishing productive relationships with team members.

Develops the expertise to successfully:
- Guide teams in holding productive meetings.
- Provide helpful feedback to teams on their work.
- Move teams to the next level of collaboration when needed.
- Read and respond appropriately to team logs.
- Establish online communication among teams; and between teams, designated school and district leaders, and consultants.
- Model leading a team meeting, if necessary.
- Troubleshoot team problems as they arise.
- Help with team logistics to the extent possible (gather needed resources; teach a class to allow a teacher to observe a colleague, etc.).
- Observe classroom applications of teaching practices that teachers are working on collaboratively and provide productive feedback.
- Provide books and/or research-based information on topics teams are studying.

- Provide updates on the team's work to the principal, outside consultants, and others as requested.
- Set up webinars and other types of online networking as a way of connecting team members with outside consultants for coaching and troubleshooting.
- Assist in seeing that team members respond to surveys and help with other formative data collection as needed.
- Regularly publicize the work of the teams (through wikis, school web sites, newsletters, bulletin boards, PTA meetings, faculty meetings, etc.).
- Recognize and advocate for needed changes in the school organization that will better promote and support teacher collaboration.

Builds the knowledge and skill to:
- Train new teachers in the professional learning team process.
- Do follow-up training with existing teams as needed.
- Lead training sessions for other faculties as needed.

Tool 10.2: Organize for the journey

Directions: Good facilitation begins with good organization. Set up a method to collect and organize information before the team start-up. Keep on hand this list of types of information and artifacts a facilitator might maintain throughout the professional learning team process, and review it periodically to be sure you are covering the team's needs.

INFORMATION:

1. **Teams:** Record team members' names, information about each (subject taught, special skills and training, etc.), and contact information. See Tool 7.1 for one method of gathering information about team members.

2. **Logistical information:** Keep a record of when teams will meet, where they will meet, and how long meetings are scheduled to last.

3. **Team goals:** Keep each team's goal in a place where you can easily access it while reading logs, briefly visiting a meeting, and so on.

4. **Team logs and communications:** Set up a separate folder, a notebook section, or electronic folder for each team. Keep a record of each team's communications there. Include copies of all team logs as well as feedback sent to teams in response to their logs. Add other communications concerning the team's work.

5. **Reports and memos:** Include copies of any reports you make on a team's progress or of the professional learning team project in general. These records might include informal memos to the team members, principal, etc.

6. **Resources:** Keep a record of materials (research articles, books, web sites, DVDs, outside experts, etc.) that team members use in their study and work.

7. **Monitoring and evaluation:** Include team self-assessments, pre-assessments, mid-year evaluations, and end-of-the-year evaluations, plus other input and observations. Include anecdotal data, such as agendas from faculty meetings, showing changes in school faculty meetings as professional learning teams gain higher priority, for example. Include information on changes in classroom instruction, changes in teachers' behaviors, and any signs that teacher collaboration across the school is increasing.

8. **Tools and tips:** Keep track of tools, tips, and ideas that further the team's progress. These can inform future professional learning team work.

9. **Personal journal:** Keep a journal of your own activities and reflections. Soon you'll have an understandable history of the project and a source of invaluable information for later use. Journaling may seem like a nuisance at first, but it's a great way to document the project's evolution. Your daily reflections will spur valuable personal insights and help steer your future course.

Tool 10.3: Build rapport with teams

Directions: These 10 categories of actions can help the facilitator build and maintain good relationships with team members. Expand on the list as you work with teams. Included with each category is a space to reflect and record what you are doing or have done to build relationships with team members in that specific area.

Relationship-building behaviors and ideas

Show an interest in team members.

Some ideas:

- Call team members by name.
- Learn something about their families, interests, hobbies, and aspirations, and use this information to personalize conversations when you talk with them.
- Take time to mention something they told you in a previous conversation. (To help you recall information, carry a small notebook and make notes in it.)
- Be attentive as they speak.
- Send birthday cards and recognize big events in team members' lives.

What I'm doing in this area

_____

_____

_____

_____

_____

_____

Relationship-building behaviors and ideas

Be an effective listener.

Some ideas:

- Face the person speaking, lean forward slightly, and make eye contact.
- Respond. Your responses can be both verbal and nonverbal, such as nodding, smiling, etc. When you respond, speak with the same energy level as the person speaking.
- Concentrate on what the person is saying. Listen for what team members mean as well as what they say.
- Do not think about what to say next while listening to someone. Give that person your full attention.
- Do not interrupt. A quick way to destroy trust and rapport is to interrupt while a person is speaking.

What I'm doing in this area

_____

_____

_____

_____

_____

_____

Relationship-building behaviors and ideas

Spend time informally in team members' classrooms.

Some ideas:

- Gain insight into their teaching styles and any innovative strategies team members are using. Then reference the good things they are doing when you stop by a team meeting, during a faculty meeting, and at other times you have opportunities to offer kudos to team members.
- Offer to videotape a teacher using a strategy the team developed so that team members can examine the videotaped lesson during a team meeting.

What I'm doing in this area

_____

_____

_____

_____

_____

_____

_____

_____

Relationship-building behaviors and ideas

Establish ways for teams to network.

Some ideas:

- Set up an electronic folder for each team containing e-mail addresses for team members. Make these folders available to all teams and invite them to use these as a location for sharing teaching ideas.
- If you're an off-campus facilitator, invite teams to send you copies of their logs electronically, and respond by e-mail.
- Set up an online site such as a wiki (or have a student do this) where teams can post resources, updates about team members, teaching tips, student successes, and other community-building information.

What I'm doing in this area

_____

_____

_____

_____

_____

_____

Relationship-building behaviors and ideas

Stay in frequent contact.

Some ideas:

- Periodically send articles and information to team members electronically.
- Connect teachers to high-quality education web sites, and involve them in exploring resources that exist beyond the school site. (See Tool 8.11.)

What I'm doing in this area

_____

_____

_____

_____

_____

_____

_____

_____

_____

Relationship-building behaviors and ideas

Be mindful of your body language.

Some ideas:

- Unfold your arms, and remember to smile.
- Watch your tone of voice, facial expression, repetitive movements, and muscle tension.
- Remember to make eye contact and show genuine interest.
- Smile a lot.
- Avoid looking down or fiddling with objects.
- Keep your body relaxed.

What I'm doing in this area

_____

_____

_____

_____

_____

_____

Relationship-building behaviors and ideas

Exhibit the same qualities you value in others.

Some ideas:

- Be dependable.
- Be respectful.
- Be friendly and positive.
- Do what you say you will do.
- Exhibit honesty, integrity, and follow-through.

What I'm doing in this area

_____
_____
_____
_____
_____
_____
_____
_____

Relationship-building behaviors and ideas

Do not take team reactions personally.

Some ideas:

- Expect that change of any kind will cause some degree of turmoil and resistance.
- Practice keeping an objective mental stance regarding team members' comments and responses.
- Avoid personalizing comments. Imagine that you are looking down on the situation from a balcony and analyzing it. Do not label the situation as "good" or "bad." Instead, just think to yourself: "This is interesting. I wonder what this is all about." This exercise will help you retain an analytical viewpoint that will prove more effective in working with teams.

What I'm doing in this area

_____
_____
_____
_____
_____
_____

Relationship-building behaviors and ideas

Relax and give it time.

Some ideas:

- Understand that building relationships takes time, persistence, and energy.
- Accept that you will not know all answers.
- Apologize if you make a mistake, and remain grounded in the basic principles of good professional learning team work.
- Relax and be yourself as you work with teams.

What I'm doing in this area

_____
_____
_____
_____
_____
_____
_____
_____

Relationship-building behaviors and ideas

Show appreciation.

Some ideas:

- Provide team members with personal business cards.
- Send faculty memos to call attention to good things teams are doing.
- Provide teachers with a surprise luncheon.
- Hold occasional drawings for a team gift for teams with perfect attendance.
- Take pictures of teachers meeting together, trying new teaching strategies, and engaging in other team events. Post the photos on school bulletin boards, or use them in newsletters.
- Take photos of students (with permission) from each team member's class. Look at the pictures during team meetings to motivate teachers and remind them of the importance of their learning team work.
- Create surprise baskets of office supplies or snacks for teams.
- Provide team members with a duty-free lunch.

What I'm doing in this area

_____
_____

Tool 10.4: A sample professional learning team agreement

Directions: Use this example of an agreement between a facilitator and members of a professional learning team to work with team members to clarify both your own role as facilitator and expectations for team members. After modifying this example or writing your own agreement, be sure that you and each team get a copy of the completed agreement.

LEARNING TEAM GOAL

To increase student learning in our goal area, we will work together weekly throughout the school year to add to our knowledge and teaching expertise in this area. The school administration will actively encourage the learning team process by providing resources, time, and support.

The facilitator will:

1. Assist team members in building their skills in working together in professional learning teams.
2. Assist the professional learning teams with logistics, troubleshooting, and specific areas of need.
3. Provide regular feedback when requested.
4. Spotlight the team's work in the school community.
5. Provide the team with resources for research and information as needed.
6. Read and respond to team logs.
7. Collect data and information about the changes that occur as a result of the team's work during the year.

Learning team members will:

1. Actively participate in the professional learning team during the school year.
2. Keep a positive attitude and persist in moving the team's work forward.
3. Study and experiment with new teaching approaches to help students learn.
4. Systematically monitor how the team's work is making a difference for students, teachers, and the school.
5. Keep team logs of team discussions and decisions.
6. Share logs schoolwide and read logs that other teams share.
7. Provide productive feedback and recommendations regarding the professional learning team process.

Tool 10.5: Information checklist for facilitators

Directions: This checklist can give the facilitator a quick picture of a team over time and an idea of where to intervene to help teams progress. Keep periodic tabs on the team's progress. Check the box next to each item according to your impression of the team's work. **Yes** means you clearly observed this behavior. **No** means that team members had an opportunity to exhibit this behavior but did not do so. **NA** indicates that team members had no opportunity to exhibit this behavior. (For example, the team plan may not call for teachers to review and study research at a particular meeting.) Add comments to help you remember and track progress, then use the information to intervene and help team members increase their skills and productivity when needed, using your wisdom and tools from previous steps.

Team _____   **Date** _____

Behaviors	Yes	No	NA	Comments
1. The team meets regularly.				
2. During the meeting, all discussions center on the team's focus.				
3. The team keeps the same focus from meeting to meeting.				
4. Learning team meetings differ from department or grade-level meetings.				
5. The atmosphere at team meetings is relaxed and friendly.				
6. Team members follow the norms they established.				
7. Roles and responsibilities rotate among team members.				
8. Team members demonstrate skill in working together.				
9. Team members are studying research and information in their focus area.				
10. Team members are learning more about effective ways of teaching students.				
11. Team members are developing and applying new instructional strategies.				
12. Team members monitor and discuss the results of their work in terms of both teacher progress and student progress.				
13. Team members are gaining new understanding of their students.				
14. The team keeps logs of each team meeting that contain big ideas from discussions and decisions.				
15. Team members are communicating their work to others outside the team.				

Tool 10.6: Professional learning teams that work

Directions: Share this list of characteristics of schools that have produced effective professional learning teams and seen positive changes in classroom instruction and student learning with other school leaders, including teacher leaders, to determine what characteristics are present in your school. Next, decide what steps leaders might take to create desired characteristics.

A professional learning team that works:

Has a supportive context and:

- ❑ Meets at the school.
- ❑ Meets during the school day.
- ❑ Has sufficient time, support, and resources to enable teachers to master new content and pedagogy and to integrate these into their practice.
- ❑ Is sustained over time, allowing teachers to integrate new knowledge and strategies into their practices and to reflect on the experience.

Is planned in advance and:

- ❑ Is driven by analyses of student-learning data.
- ❑ Is driven by a coherent long-term plan.
- ❑ Is collaboratively developed with teachers and those who will participate in and facilitate that development.
- ❑ Includes intentional follow-up and support.
- ❑ Provides resources to support teacher learning and collaboration.
- ❑ Builds in accountability practices and evaluation of professional development programs to provide a foundation for future planning.

Produces outcomes and:

- ❑ Enhances teachers' content and pedagogic knowledge.
- ❑ Enhances teachers' understanding of how their students learn.
- ❑ Prepares teachers to make informed decisions about instruction.
- ❑ Results in more accomplished teaching.

- ❑ Promotes collegiality and collaboration.
- ❑ Promotes an attitude of continuous inquiry and improvement.
- ❑ Contributes to measurable improvement in student achievement.
- ❑ Contributes to a professional culture in which teachers develop a common understanding of accomplished teaching.

A school that produces successful professional learning teams:

Meets teacher learning needs and:

- ❑ Provides teachers with the knowledge and skills to collaborate productively.
- ❑ Deepens educators' content knowledge, providing them with research-based instructional strategies to help students meet rigorous academic standards.
- ❑ Prepares teachers to use various classroom assessments appropriately.
- ❑ Builds deeper insight into how students learn in their particular context.
- ❑ Builds a clear, well-defined image of effective classroom learning and teaching.
- ❑ Prepares educators to understand and appreciate all students and to have high expectations for their academic achievement.
- ❑ Aligns with the curriculum and assessments in use in the setting.

Supports ongoing teacher growth and:

❑ Focuses on teachers as central to student learning.

❑ Allows time for teachers to engage in meaningful discussion, planning, and practice.

❑ Provides resources for teachers to refine and expand their pedagogical repertoire and their content knowledge.

❑ Provides comfortable, respectful meeting environments conducive to adult learning.

❑ Monitors its own progress, provides its members with effective feedback, and helps team members sustain momentum.

Supports team activities and:

❑ Makes available student performance and achievement data — including student feedback, teacher observation, analysis of student work, and test scores— to help teachers determine where to focus their collective efforts.

❑ Affords teachers with time and opportunities to develop new understandings and skills, and to broaden their teaching approaches to create better learning for students.

❑ Provides for and promotes continuous inquiry, experimentation, and reflection about instruction.

❑ Includes occasions for team members to observe and be observed teaching.

❑ Provides teachers with research-based information and resources.

❑ Supplies effective and regular feedback to teams.

Assesses the impact of professional learning teams on:

❑ Teachers' knowledge and skills.

❑ Teachers' attitudes and motivation.

❑ Classroom practices.

❑ Student learning.

❑ Productive teaming.

Evaluates and:

❑ Involves continuous assessments.

❑ Uses multiple sources of data and information.

❑ Uses data to guide teacher growth and team efforts.

Provides capable leadership and:

❑ Respects and nurtures teachers' professional and leadership capacity.

❑ Guides continuous instructional improvement.

❑ Respects teachers as professional, adult lifelong learners.

❑ Uses teachers' expertise, cultivates leaders, and involves teachers in planning.

❑ Applies knowledge about adult learning and change.

Tool 10.7: Is this a good policy?

Directions: Policies in place in schools today often have existed for decades. Periodically revisiting school policies and operating procedures can be eye-opening and can pave the way to creating fresh policies that better accomplish goals of openness, trust, and productive professional collaboration.

Use these questions with other school leaders, including teacher leaders, to discuss specific policies and procedures in place at your school. These may include both written policies and traditional ways of working. (For example, some administrators highly structure teachers' meeting times.)

Place an X along the continuum beneath each question to indicate what you think about the policy. Then discuss your perceptions of this policy as a group. If the policy does not help build a collaborative school culture with shared leadership and vision, then discuss how to begin making needed policy changes.

1. Does the policy/procedure reduce teachers' isolation, or does it perpetuate the traditional policy of working alone?

   Perpetuates isolation   **Reduces isolation**

2. Does the policy provide schedules and structures that keep teachers who teach the same students in close proximity with one another?

   Perpetuates separateness   **Promotes close proximity**

3. Does the policy encourage teachers to assume the role of learners, or does it reward customary teacher-as-expert approaches to teaching and learning?

   Teacher as expert   **Teacher as learner**

4. Does the policy reward individuals or teams?

   Rewards individuals   **Rewards teams**

5. Does the policy establish an environment of professional trust and encourage problem solving, or does it encourage hiding problems?

   Defensive environment   **Trusting environment**

6. Does the policy make it possible to restructure time and space within schools, or are new forms of teaching and learning expected to emerge within traditional structures?

....

Traditional use of time and space   **Reorganized use of time and space**

7. Does the policy encourage a focus on teacher professional growth and learning that gives priority to teachers learning why and how, or does it emphasize teachers following prescribed teaching patterns?

....

Prescribed teaching patterns   **Teacher learning and growth**

8. Does the policy encourage a risk-free environment for experimenting with new ways of teaching?

....

Cautious environment   **Risk-free environment**

9. Does the policy support teachers' use of multiple methods of communication?

....

No focus on communication   **Supports a variety of communication methods**

10. Does the policy provide greater autonomy for teachers?

....

Teaching driven by external guidelines   **Teachers use professional wisdom**

11. Does the policy empower teachers to be genuine decision makers?

....

Administrators make decisions   **Teachers share in decision making**

12. Does the policy foster collaboration rather than competitiveness?

....

Competitiveness   **Collaboration**

Tool 10.8: How important are you?

Directions: Read the first three statements on this sheet to yourself. Then read and discuss the three research findings at the bottom of the page. Brainstorm a list of ways school leaders might accomplish these actions. Then compile a list of actions you will take to provide successful professional learning team leadership.

Successful leadership of professional learning teams involves:

1. Setting a clear direction so that faculty members develop shared understandings about the school and its goals. Develop a clear direction to help faculty members make sense of their professional learning team work.
2. Developing people. Provide individualized team support and encouragement through direct feedback and contact with each professional learning team.
3. Redesigning the school. Organizational conditions sometimes wear down teachers' good intentions and actually prevent professional learning teams from doing their work. Examine your school policies to identify and revise those that hinder collaboration and take the focus off quality instruction.

A look at the research

A 2004 study commissioned by the Wallace Foundation, *How Leadership Influences Student Learning,* points to leadership as a major factor in student learning. The major findings include:

- Leadership is second only to classroom teaching in its impact on student achievement. What leaders do (directly and indirectly) accounts for about 25% of total school effects.
- Leadership effects are largest where and when they are needed most. Studies demonstrate that the effects of successful leadership are much greater in schools that are challenged by difficult circumstances.
- Leadership has a positive impact on achievement when the leader focuses on changes that improve classroom practice and understands the magnitude of the change being undertaken.

> **"To improve schools, improve leadership. Indeed, there are virtually no documented instances of troubled schools being turned around without intervention by a powerful leader. Many other factors may contribute to such turnarounds, but leadership is the catalyst."**
>
> — *Kenneth Leithwood, Karen Seashore Louis, Stephen Anderson, and Kyla Wahlstrom (2004)*

Source: Adapted from *How Leadership Influences Student Learning,* by Kenneth Leithwood, Karen Seashore Louis, Stephen Anderson, and Kyla Wahlstrom. (2004). Center for Applied Research and Educational Improvement and Ontario Institute for Studies in Education, pp. 5-9.

Tool 10.9: What's a leader to do?

Directions: Consider how you would accomplish each of these ideas to support professional learning teams.

1. **Understand** what a fully functioning professional learning team looks like.

2. **Promote** teachers' beliefs in the benefits of working together and in their ability to do so productively.

3. **Arrange** the school schedule to allow for meetings during the school day.

4. **Be aware** of teachers' levels of commitment, and support full, active participation in professional learning teams.

5. **Involve** teachers in making decisions about professional learning teams.

6. **Give** teachers opportunities to meet and to observe one another's classes as they implement new strategies.

7. **Provide** rewards and recognitions for teams rather than for individuals.

8. **Provide** gestures of appreciation (surprise baskets, supplies, business cards, coupons, duty-free lunch, etc.).

9. **Remove** a noninstructional duty.

10. **Give** teachers permission to take risks and try new teaching approaches.

11. **Provide** team members with professional learning credit.

12. **Allow** teachers to tie learning teams to personal growth plans.

13. **Give** professional learning teams high visibility schoolwide.

14. **Provide** regular and productive feedback to teams.

15. **Maintain** a strong, observable commitment to professional learning teams.

> **"Leadership appears to be the art of getting others to want to do something you are convinced should be done."**
> — *Vance Packard, author*

> **"Leadership is practiced not so much in words as in attitude and actions."**
> — *Harold S. Geneen, founder, MCI Communications*

Tool 10.10: Sample note from an administrator

Directions: Use this sample note of how one administrator provided initial direction to a group of teams as they began the learning team process, adapting it as needed for your situation. Use the example to generate ideas for how you and other leaders will provide guidance, visibility, and a sense of importance to this professional learning team work.

Hi, professional learning teams:

I look forward to this new adventure!

1.   Please decide on a regular meeting schedule (day, date, and time) for your team meetings. Send this information, along with the names of everyone on your team, to the facilitator, who will then send it to me.

2.   Remember, your professional learning team is not a team planning meeting. The focus must be on a specific instructional area that team members would like to investigate, implement, and evaluate. For example, math, science, and social studies teachers might examine reading strategies across content areas and develop a tool kit of common strategies to help students improve their understanding of written text. Communications teachers may want to focus on balanced literacy using the materials from your workshop this summer.

3.   Whenever you hold a meeting, choose a recorder. That person should capture the following information: who was present, how long the meeting lasted, and the date. He or she should also record briefly the major discussion points and what was decided or the outcome of the meeting. This log should be in a Word document and attached to an e-mail.

4.   The log should be sent directly to all members of the professional learning team, the principal, the facilitator, and me as soon as possible following your meeting. The easiest thing to do is for everyone to set up a professional learning team group in your personal address book.

I plan to visit teams whenever I can. I will also respond to your logs. Please do not hesitate to contact me if you have questions or need resources.

Sincerely,
Dr. Howard

Ask Dr. Developer: Honoring all voices crucial in consensus

Q: I'm all for getting everybody on the school improvement team to agree with a decision. But what do you do when you've got a couple of stubborn people who just won't go along with the group?

A: This is the $64,000 question of the Reaching Consensus Challenge. Individuals who block consensus are likely to feel as if they haven't been heard by the group. They probably aren't objecting to the whole solution, just to part of it. Your mission is to ensure that their concerns are heard and that the group responds to them.

Here's a series of questions the facilitator can ask to help move the group toward consensus.

- Under what conditions would you support this solution?
- What part of the solution do you oppose?
- What parts of the solution would you modify so you'd be more comfortable with the solution?
- What would be necessary for you to agree with this solution?
- Would you be willing to live with the solution for a limited time?
- What would be a reasonable time before we reassess the decision?
- Under what conditions would you be willing to put aside your differences?

In addition, ask the team members who support the recommendation:

- What are you willing to do to adjust your views to respond to the discomfort of those who are

Ask Dr. Developer
Dr. Developer has all the answers to questions that staff developers ask. (At least he thinks he does!)

not yet in agreement?

- If you were not in agreement, what parts of the solution might be troublesome to you?

One caution: Individuals who feel as if they haven't been heard can become uncomfortable by being singled out for this kind of attention. The facilitator needs to be sensitive to that issue as well.

These can be frustrating moments. Try to keep in perspective that whole school systems may struggle with similar issues. As you discover how to deal with this challenge, you'll be learning a great deal that can be applied to other, even larger, debates in your district and state.

Source: "Honoring all voices crucial in consensus," by Joan Richardson. (1997, October/November). *Tools for Schools, 8.*

About the author

Anne Jolly is an educational consultant who works with national organizations, states, districts, and schools to design and implement professional learning teams. As president of PLTWorks, Jolly develops  educational materials and provides training and support to assist educators in implementing and sustaining professional learning teams. Her primary focus is providing practical, how-to help for engaging teachers in sustained, on-site professional development through collaborative learning and action.

Jolly has worked as project director for Teacher Collaboration with the SERVE Center at the University of North Carolina at Greensboro. Before that, she taught science for 16 years in the Mobile (Ala.) County Public Schools and worked with special assistance teams with the Alabama State Department of Education. She has served on several national commissions and panels, including the National Commission on Math and Science Teaching for the 21st Century (the Glenn Commission), the National Academy of Sciences Committee on K-12 Science Education, and the National Steering Committee for America Goes Back to School.

Jolly is an author, a former Alabama Teacher of the Year, a member of the Alabama Governor's Commission on Quality Teaching, and a member of the Board of Directors for the Alabama Math, Science, and Technology Education Coalition.